M000020724

Shaping
My
Hat

by Jake Billingsley

Library of Congress Cataloging-in-Publication Data

Billingsley, Jake, 1941-
  Shaping my hat / by Jake Billingsley.
    p. cm.
  ISBN 1-59822-006-3 (pbk.)
  1. Billingsley, Jake, 1941- 2. Entertainers—United States—Biography.
  I. Title.
  PN2287.B4546A3 2005
  791.4502'8'092--dc22   2005012582

Printed in the United States of America

ISBN-10: 1-59822-006-3
ISBN-13: 978-1-59822-006-3
2 4 6 8 10 9 7 5 3
0405

All inquiries for volume purchases of this book should be
addressed to Wordware Publishing, Inc. at
2320 Los Rios Boulevard
Plano, Texas 75074

Telephone inquiries may be made by calling:
(972) 423-0090

Dedication

This book is dedicated to my mama and daddy, Erma and J.T. Billingsley, who, despite never experiencing monetary success, were the most successful people I have ever known. They gave so much of themselves to others, not for reward, but because they truly lived with love in their hearts. Simply put, my mama and daddy are my special heroes. They helped me in every way a parent can possibly help a child. The lessons they taught, by example, include respect, effort, self-confidence, and, most of all, unconditional love.

Foreword

by Jeni Billingsley

As Jake and I travel around the country I am constantly asked the same question: "You know him best. What is Jake *really* like?"

The answer really is quite simple. He is nothing more and nothing less than what he appears to be. Jake is an interesting character and totally authentic. He is comfortable in his own shirt.

He is as tough as a boot but as gentle as a lamb. I watched him sew up a cut on his hand with a needle and thread. I was with him when he set his own badly broken leg. I watched him walk down the hall of a hospital one hour after spinal surgery. I was there when a horse rolled over him on the side of a mountain. I have seen him outwork men half his age. I laughed when marathon runners called him a "mutant guide" because he walked them into the ground in the mountains.

He is emotional about things he loves: his family, nature, good movies, and anything spiritual. He is tender and compassionate about life and people. He loves deeply, purely, and unconditionally. He takes time with children, and they truly love him because they instinctively know he is real.

He is a leader. People follow him because he is good and fair. His management style is laissez-faire and he will work side by side with his employees. As a result, they will do anything for him.

Two words describe him best. He is the "eternal optimist." He tackles every challenge with enthusiasm and a positive attitude. He loves a challenge and is totally focused on the job until he thinks it is complete.

His greatest strength — and greatest weakness — is his perseverance. Jake just won't give up if he believes in the effort. Sometimes there is success and sometimes failure, but that never stops him.

He dislikes bullies and those who try to intimidate others. All persons are equal to him, and that is one of his greatest assets. He is fair, honest, straightforward, and respects others and their opinions.

He is an adventurer, a risk-taker, and the best storyteller ever. People are mesmerized by tales of his exciting adventures.

He believes life is about doing your best, conquering your fears, and learning about yourself in the process. He believes that failures can be the greatest teachers if you learn the lesson.

I had to convince Jake to write this book because his fans kept asking for a "book about Jake," and finally he agreed. He loves to write, but his passion is western love stories so this book was difficult. He wrote another book, *Coogan*, years ago but never attempted to have it published because, in his own words, "I wrote it because I wanted to. If no one else likes it, so what?"

In this book, *Shaping My Hat*, Jake gives the reader an insight into his life. It is much more than a biography. It is an experience, chock full of **lessons on how to be a better person and live a better life**. The book will cause you to laugh and make you cry, but most of all, it will inspire you to **Shape Your Hat**.

In summary, Jake is the most genuine man I have ever met, and I would eat bugs for him any day.

Acknowledgments

For as long as I can remember I have loved to put my ideas on paper. That simple process of writing has helped me reinforce those ideas by giving them energy. As I continue to write, the ideas expand and take on a shape all their own.

The book *Shaping My Hat* started as a simple idea: A number of people said they would like to read a story about my life. As I began to write my autobiography the idea was reinforced and energized.

It was an effort for me to write in first person and I became discouraged. Special people gave me the courage to continue, and the idea was transformed from a book about Jake to a book about life lessons.

To these special people I would like to say thank you.

My two wonderful children, Jamie and Jay, whose continued love and support will always motivate me.

My darlin' Jeni, whose presence in my life makes me want to be a better person.

Alan and Martha McCuller, who helped me in so many ways to get the book published.

Vivian Adams, who helped me with the title and cover for this book.

Phyllis Firebaugh, who gave me the necessary push when I wanted to give up.

Wendy Cosper, for her suggestions and support.

A special thanks to the fans of the television show *Survivor* who continue to be a constant source of inspiration to me.

Introduction

My biography, *Shaping My Hat*, begins at a time in my life where nothing seemed to be going right. I was in complete despair when I took a journey into the San Juan Mountains of Colorado, removed my clothes, except for my beat-up old cowboy hat, and looked for the meaning of life. The book *Shaping My Hat* is a metaphor for shaping my life as it takes the reader through a series of adventures and life-changing events as I attempt to uncover the real Jake. The book is an internal journey into the essence of my character as I struggle to find my true identity while facing the harsh and ever-changing outside world.

Complacent people are hereby forewarned:
Do not attempt to read this book unless you
want the inspiration to shape a better life.

About Jake:

 Jake Billingsley, a native Texan, was born in Tyler and raised in Texarkana. His background is as interesting as the man himself. He has done everything from developing real estate in the Dallas metroplex to hunting grizzly bear in Siberia with a bow and arrow. He is as comfortable in the boardrooms of large corporations as he is in the wilderness, having served as senior officer of several large real estate companies and guided big game hunters as president of Rocky Mountain Outfitters.

Jake has a bachelor of science degree from Texas A&M and prior to his real estate career worked as a rancher, county agent, and for Texas Power and Light Company. He loves to write and is currently writing a weekly column for the *Sherman Democrat*. He also loves to compete, is an avid Masters swimmer, and has competed in numerous triathlons in past years. It's no wonder CBS picked Jake to be on the award-winning television show *Survivor: Thailand* at age sixty.

Jake, a popular speaker with an enthusiastic delivery, has appeared on numerous television and radio shows and in a number of television commercials. He plays Sheriff Jimmy in the movie *After Sundown*.

Chapter 1

"I went to the woods because I wished to live deliberately... and see if I could not learn what it had to teach, and not, when I came to die, to discover that I had not lived. I wanted to live deep and suck out all the marrow of life... to put to rout all that was not life..."

Henry David Thoreau

THE BAY GELDING stopped and moved off the trail, grabbing a mouthful of high meadow grass in the process. I loosened the reins and let him munch. Glancing at my watch through tear-stained eyes, I determined that it had been four hours since I said goodbye to my best friend, Dirk Ross, at the corral.

"How long you gonna be up there?" he asked.

"As long as it takes."

"When you get to where you're going, just tie the bridle to the saddle and let him go. He'll find his way back down."

I only had a general idea of where I was, and it mattered not in the least. I had started the horse up the steep East Creek Trail but had paid absolutely no attention to his route. It did not matter to me. Rather, I gave the horse his head and only occasionally urged him over a log or through a creek.

The year was 1989 and it was only three days before my forty-eighth birthday. The mid-August sky was clouding up and I knew we were in for a blow. Yesterday I had filed the instrument in Dallas. Today I was going into the mountains… alone. I would stay as long as it took.

Sleet began to fall, slowly at first, but then harder and harder. My beat-up old cowboy hat was now coated with it. Still, I sat in the saddle, oblivious to where I was. I lifted my arm, tucked my nose toward my shoulder, and used the fabric from my sleeve to drag the tears from my face. I looked around.

The dim trail the horse had been following cut across the meadow in front of me and into dark timber on the other side of the meadow. Downhill to my right I could see a number of large spruce trees growing on a ridge surrounded by meadow. Instinctively I urged the horse in that direction. On either side of the spruce were valleys that continued downward. About a thousand yards ahead they abruptly changed and I could just make out a vertical cliff through the spruce. Through the noise of the sleet I could hear the trickle of water to my left.

"Spring," I thought to myself.

The bay continued down the slope, then started up to the grove. The ground flattened at the grove, dropping off on either side into the valleys that made up the meadow. Picking our way through the huge boulders that were everywhere, we stopped under the canopy of a hundred-foot blue spruce. Here the sleet no longer pelted us. I dismounted. This was the place I was supposed to be.

"I'm here," I said aloud, more to myself than to my horse. "Probably somewhere just shy of 10,000 feet."

I untied the bedroll from the saddle and tossed it next to the trunk of the spruce, then unbridled the bay, tied the bridle to the saddle, and said quietly, "Thanks, boy." The bay moved off into the meadow and began to crop the grass. I knew he would head back to the corral when he had filled his belly.

I removed my hat and banged it against my right thigh, knocking the half-inch of snow and sleet from its weathered brim and crown. I loved that old hat. It had protected me once again from the elements.

That hat had floated down rivers — sometimes on my head, sometimes in the water. I had worn it climbing mountains all over the United States. It had been on beaches and in deserts. It had been under mule trains and down ski slopes. It had a hole where Steve Williams shot it with an arrow and a sewed-up place just under the hatband where a tree limb had punctured it on a dark night. That old hat had character... character that came from adventure. I remembered the time I had taken it in to get cleaned, reblocked, and reshaped.

"Would you sell that hat?" the cowboy behind the counter asked.

"Never have thought about it," I answered truthfully. "Why do you ask?"

"Well, I have people in here all the time looking for a real cowboy's hat and they pay top dollar. That old hat has character, and people pay for character. I could probably get you $250 or $300 for that old hat as it is. If I clean and block it, it won't be worth near as much."

"If this hat is worth that much, I guess I will just have to leave it the way it is. It does have character."

The sleet stopped and the sun came out. "Not unusual for the San Juans," I thought. "Especially in August. One minute a blizzard, the next, sunshine."

My shoulders slumped forward and I sat under the spruce. I looked at the bay still cropping grass. Suddenly I began to sob. Huge tears rolled down my cheeks. There was no stopping them. I'm not sure I wanted to.

Sometime later I stood and removed all my clothes except for my beat-up old hat. It was cold, but I seemed to be oblivious as I walked down the slope toward the spring. I moved slowly... deliberately. My shoulders were hunched forward and my head was bowed. A gust of wind whistled through the trees and I could feel its cold breath on my shoulders and back. I knelt down on the soft mossy ground and drank my fill of the clean fresh mountain water that cascaded off a large rock and into a small clear pool.

Lying in the tall meadow grass I watched as the ever-lengthening shadows worked their way down the slope to the place where I lay. Soon they covered me as they found their way past the spring and up the other side of the draw. Remnants of the sun could still be seen on the tree line on top of the ridge, but I knew in a few minutes it too would be gone. Dusk was bringing with it the cold night air as it blanketed me, causing me to shake uncontrollably. I angrily clambered to my feet and stumbled back to the spruce, crawled in my sleeping bag, and promptly fell asleep.

It was probably midmorning when I woke. It was rare indeed for the sun to rise before me in the mornings. I have always been an early riser. No real reason but my mama used to say, "Early to bed, early to rise, makes a man healthy, wealthy, and wise."

I did not want to wake up. It was far too painful to be conscious. In sleep I could find sanctuary from the grief.

Once again I could feel my eyes begin to water. I gathered a pen and pad I had stored in the bottom of my bedroll, walked into the sunlit meadow, and sat on a large boulder. The healing energy of the sun felt good on my naked body. It was here I began to go over my life from the beginning. I was looking for answers in the only place I knew I could find them… in me… in the mountains.

I hoped to find the answers by going through my forty-eight years page by page, starting at the beginning. I planned to record as many key events as I could remember. I was determined to stay as long as it took. When I left the mountains I hoped to have answers… answers to simple questions. If not complete answers, I wanted to at least have a plan of action to help me find the answers in the future. I had plenty of questions… questions of depth. Questions like, Who am I? and Why am I here? I felt I was a prisoner in my own body. It seemed to me that I had been living someone else's life. Not mine.

The hats I had worn all through my life had been shaped by my desire to please other people. I had shaped a son hat, a scout hat, a student hat, a husband hat, a provider hat, and a father hat. I wanted to shape my own hat for a change. I wanted to find the real Jake.

"Who am I, why am I here, and what am I here to do?" I said aloud.

It was a question that was gnawing at me and a question I hoped to answer. I wanted to find the shape of my own hat and wear it for the rest of my life.

In the times in my life that I had failures, I had always attempted to learn more about myself. It would have been so much easier to blame something or someone else, but I was not looking for the easy way out. My parents had taught me that in every failure there was a lesson to be learned.

"Adversity doesn't build character, it's how one handles adversity that builds character. If at first you don't succeed, try, try again." My mother must have said that to me over a thousand times when I was growing up.

I wanted to grow. I wanted to become a better person. I figured that the current grief and despair that I was experiencing was for a reason. I had something to learn from it. What was it? It was a time to be quiet and listen. It was a time to get back to nature. It was a time to take stock of myself. It was a time to reflect on the past and plan for the future. That was what I had come to do. Take stock. It was to be a voyage into me. I knew I was on a journey to discover myself, who I am, and what I stand for. It was to be an expedition into my higher self... a time for inner perspective... a time to talk to God. My failures, despair, and grief led me here. Because of them I was at this place at this time. I accepted the responsibility of the choices I had made throughout my life and the consequences of those choices. Why shouldn't I accept that responsibility? They had been my choices. Some had been good, some not so good, but they had been my choices and my consequences.

I was seeking answers and I knew the answers I sought would come. I also knew it was up to me to find the answers. No one else was responsible for me but me. Nobody else could make me happy. I was on my own.

My plan was simple: I would begin by writing about me. I would try to remember all the significant events in my life. By reflecting on where I had been I felt I could move forward with clarity. I knew the peace of the mountains would help me find what I was looking for. And so I began at the beginning. My pen touched the pad and I began to write.

I was born on August 21, 1941, in Tyler, Texas, right in the middle of World War II where over fifty million people lost their lives. I was given the name Jake Thomas Billingsley. On the day I was born German forces, under Hitler, cut the railroad between Leningrad and Moscow. Four months later the Japanese attacked Pearl Harbor.

My parents were Erma Walker Billingsley and Julius Thomas Billingsley. Dad, who went by J.T. or Jake, was a detective for the Tyler police department and Mother was a clerk typist for Camp Fannin, which housed 19,000 troops. I had an older sister, Ann, and a grandmother and grandfather on my father's side and none on my mother's side. I had several uncles and aunts on my mother's side, and one uncle and one cousin on my father's side.

Astrologically speaking I am a double Leo as I was born with the sun and moon sign of Leo. I am told that because of this there is harmony between my feelings and my actions. That sounds like a good thing to me.

I was allergic to milk until age three. Today there is a name for it. It's called lactose intolerance. Back then we just bought a goat and I drank goat's milk.

I put my pad and pen on the boulder and slowly walked to the spring for a drink, taking the time to wash my face a little. Soon I was back on the boulder, pen in hand, and once again I began to write, trying not to miss a single detail.

"You had an imaginary playmate when you were a little boy," my cousin Jay had said

mockingly. "And his name was... are you ready for this... Bonnie Moore. What kind of name is that for a boy... Bonnie?"

"Leave him alone, Jay, I think it's cute," his sister Jerry took up for me.

"And Bonnie was a soldier. You used to pedal him around on your bicycle," he chided.

All his friends laughed and I didn't know what to say. I was ten when he brought it up and totally embarrassed.

A hint of a smile crossed my lips as I recalled my childhood.

We moved to Texarkana when I was three to a little house on Lumpkin Street. Daddy had always wanted to drive a train and took a job with St. Louis Southwestern Railroad, following his dream. Mother worked at Red River Army Depot, leaving Ann and me under the care of Lilly, a wonderful little black lady, during the day.

At this early age I can remember very little. I do remember my mother putting some kind of warm oil in my ears and rocking me all night. I had severe ear infections. Today, they put tubes in little ears. In the forties we just suffered.

Mama left for work at 6:30 in the morning. She arrived home at around 6:30 in the evening. How she did it I'll never know.

I remember to this day my mother reading me my favorite book, The Little Engine That Could. It was my favorite bedtime story and I took it with me everywhere I went. I slept with that book every night and my poor mother must have been tired of reading it on a daily basis.

"Chug, chug, chug. Puff, puff, puff. Ding-dong, ding-dong, ding-dong. The little train rumbled

over the tracks. She was a happy little train...
I think I can—I think I can—I think I can..."

*It was before my fourth year that Daddy was diag-
nosed with tuberculosis and was put in a sanitarium
in Shreveport, Louisiana, for rest. He stayed there
until I was about eleven. It became a circle for him.
From the sanitarium to the hospital, where he under-
went multiple lung surgeries, then back to the
sanitarium. Back and forth... sanitarium to hospital
and back again.*

*A lot of my early life is a bit fuzzy, but I remember
our chicken coop in the back yard, our goat, and my
beloved chinaberry tree.*

*When I was five my Uncle Buddy, in from the Navy,
rode to Texarkana from Houston on a Harley-
Davidson. His shirt was nearly torn off him by the
wind. I remember that so well because Uncle Buddy
and I built a tree house in that chinaberry tree.
Actually it was nothing but an old door that we
nailed between two limbs, but it became my sanctuary... my place to get away... my place to observe
others. I piloted a plane from that perch. I shot bad
guys with imaginary pistols. I watched my mother
wring the necks of chickens from the safety of my
perch. I can still smell the stench from the chicken
feathers as she dipped the chickens in boiling water
before she plucked them.*

*Another thing I remember was the fear in my
mother. Seven people were murdered in 1946 in
Texarkana. They were mostly lovers and the person
doing the killings was known as The Phantom Killer.
Mother was terrified, as we were in the house without
a man. I can remember telling her I would take care
of her and I had my trusty (toy) pistol if anything
went wrong.*

Because of my late August birthday I started the first grade younger than most. I had a great first-grade teacher. "Miss Bertha" White was the typical "old maid" schoolteacher. Her hair was in a bun every day and she didn't wear any makeup. She looked to be seven feet tall to me. Everyone in Miss Bertha's class learned to read. She absolutely made us toe the mark. I was much more into playing than reading. It didn't matter what the game, I was up for it. There were no organized sports. We just played. War... cowboys and Indians... baseball... football... dodge ball... steal the bacon. Miss Bertha, however, thought reading was the priority and I am thankful for that.

Catching birds became a priority for me. I would take some of the grain we used to feed the chickens and sprinkle it in a pile. Then I used a stick with a string tied on it to prop a cardboard box on one edge. When the bird went under the box to take a bite of the grain, I pulled the string and the box captured the bird. It was tricky business catching birds. I soon mastered the technique and was excited when I even caught a blue jay in my trap.

We had a great Christmas that first-grade year. Daddy got to come home for a couple of weeks and I was able to share with him my "Miss Bertha" reading skills. Santa Claus brought me a Daisy BB gun, and my life changed dramatically. The thing never shot far or straight, but I learned to make allowances for the gun's idiosyncrasies. The birds in the neighborhood were never safe again.

I began to laugh thinking of my first hunting days and how, at age six, I would walk down to a heavily wooded area by myself and shoot birds. I would often build a fire, pluck the birds, and eat them, although I can never remember any of them tasting very good.

It felt good to laugh and I crawled off the boulder and walked downhill toward the spring. Since I was still naked, I wondered what would happen if some poor unsuspecting rider or backpacker followed the trail into the meadow in which I was walking. It wasn't that I cared; the thought was just funny.

I could see the cliff rising through the trees in front of me as I moved farther down the slope. Then I heard a noise that I recognized immediately. It was the sound of running water. Walking toward the sound I soon saw a creek rushing over rocks, limbs, and boulders. I moved toward it as if hypnotized. The slope steepened and I slid down once on the wet grass. I stepped into the rushing water and moved with the current, watching the brook trout as they scurried out of my way. The water was icy cold and quickly numbed my feet and ankles.

Later I walked back to the boulder in the meadow. Since 1982 it had been one tough turn of events after the other. Nothing seemed to be happening right for me. My life was in turmoil... and now this... It was a bit too much. After about an hour I felt like writing.

At age seven a highly significant event happened in my life that changed me forever. Every kid on the block had a bicycle but me. I wanted one. I wanted one in the worst way.

Mom, Ann, and I went to the hospital in Shreveport. Daddy had been moved there from the sanitarium for an operation on his lungs. I didn't know it at the time but he had been given a 30% chance to pull through. Mama left me alone with him while she went out to talk to the surgeon and I broke down in a tearful plea about wanting a bicycle.

"Son, you can have a bicycle," he said weakly. My eyes lit up and he continued, "You just have to find a way to pay for it."

"What do you mean? I'm only seven."

"Son, you want the bike. Mother and I certainly can't afford to buy you one but, if you

want it bad enough, I have an idea." His voice was almost a whisper.

I moved in closer, listening intently.

He continued, "We have a lawn mower. Why don't you ask Mrs. Jackson if you can mow her yard for her? I'm sure she would pay you fifty cents to do that on a regular basis."

I could almost hear the wheels turning in my seven-year-old brain.

"Great idea. Mrs. Short needs hers mowed too, and Mrs. Lucas. I can also sell Kool-Aid on the corner."

Dad had the operation. It was a difficult one but he pulled through. The surgeons filled half his lungs with Lucite balls, which were little plastic balls about the size of Ping-Pong balls. He went back to the sanitarium for recovery and stayed there for another three and a half years.

My dad, while getting ready to go into surgery, had taught me a life lesson. Looking back on the incident I realized I was nothing but a selfish little boy. Nevertheless, my father had given me something I needed — a direction. He had sized up the strengths and weaknesses of the family, heard my objective, and helped me develop a plan. Now I had the direction. I knew what to do and how to do it.

As soon as I got back to Texarkana I began to canvass the neighborhood for yards to mow. I made a deal for six lawns at $.50 per lawn. I contracted to mow every other week. I used our old rotary push mower and a friend's grandfather taught me how to sharpen the blade with a file. At the end of two weeks I had $3.00 saved toward the bicycle.

Main Street in Texarkana had a bicycle shop. I had my bike all picked out. It was red and white, and had a horn and a shock absorber. It was the prettiest bike I had ever seen. On our next weekend trip to see Daddy he seemed overjoyed with my progress and encouraged me to continue. He whispered something to Mother and she smiled and nodded her approval.

"Son," Daddy said, "by your own effort you have made your dream of a bicycle closer to reality. You can do anything you set your mind to do. There are no dreams you can conceive that you cannot make happen. I'm proud of you, Son."

A grin broke out across my face. I was proud of my accomplishment so far and knew that the $27.00 bike would soon be mine.

Daddy continued, "Sometimes when we want things there are ways to get them that we don't think of when we start toward them. Those things just come up and we get a chance to learn more. Your mama and I have agreed on something. If you agree on it too, we will help you get that bike sooner. That is, if that is what you want."

"Of course that's what I want. You mean like quicker than saving my money and then buying it?"

Mama explained, "It's called credit, Son. That is what Daddy and I used to buy the house. We didn't have the cash to buy the house out-right so people with the money are lending it to us. We pay them back monthly. We get the use of the house and when we finish paying it off we own it ourselves. The people lending the money *get a little something extra for doing that. That something extra is called interest."*

Daddy looked me in the eye and said, "Mama and I have agreed that if you want that bike, she will go to the Schwinn dealer with you and help you establish your credit. Anyone that is old enough to push that old sickle mower around is old enough to establish credit and get his bike."

I jabbered all the way home about that bike and nearly drove Mama crazy till we went to the Schwinn dealer. While I was looking at the bike, she was talking to the owner. I saw her sign something and then the man came over to me.

"Your mother says you want to buy this bike on credit. Is that right?"

"I do. I want this bike," I said enthusiastically.

"She also tells me that you have $3.00. Am I right so far?"

"Yes, sir, I do," I said, taking my billfold out of my pocket and showing him the three one-dollar bills.

"Well now, this bicycle costs $27.00. If you give me three dollars today, that still leaves $24.00. How do you plan to pay me that $24.00?"

"I make $1.50 per week mowing lawns. I can pay you that."

"So you can pay me $1.50 per week. That seems okay with me. I'm going to charge you a little more for this bike to help me carry the note. You understand that?"

"Mama told me that was interest. I understand that."

"Okay. Now, do you know what will happen if you don't pay me back?"

"Why wouldn't I pay you back? You are doing me a favor." I looked up at Mama and she was smiling.

"I'm not doing you a favor. We are agreeing on a business arrangement. I will get paid for the bicycle plus interest. This is business. You need to be aware that if you don't pay me back as we agree, I will take the bike back."

"That will never happen," I assured him.

"Good. Now we just have one other piece of business. I am going to ask you to sign a note with me. You will be signing that you will pay me back $1.50 per week until the $24.00 plus interest is paid back. When you sign this note, you are obligating yourself to continue mowing lawns or whatever else you need to do to get the $1.50. It is your responsibility to do this. Do you understand this?"

"I do. Where do I sign?"

He handed me the note. I gave it to Mother for her to look over. She handed it back to me and I noticed that it already had her signature on it.

"Mama, you've already signed it." I looked at her.

"I just signed it as a witness to your business-men's agreement," she said with a smile.

I walked back to my bedroll, removed my hat and hung it on a broken branch, and laid down, watching the clouds through the canopy of boughs and my swollen eyes. I was in the forest again and I was by myself. Even as a child I had migrated into the forest, into a tree, or even into the bushes when I needed to work something out. There was something so soothing about being close to nature. My college days had taught me that the best way to solve any problem was to start with what I knew to be true and work through it systematically. I had found that keeping a journal handy was a good thing. Writing always helped me sort through things. Being close to the earth seemed to ground me. I had a major issue to work through.

A squirrel scolded me from a nearby pine. "What is the matter with you?" he seemed to say.

With slumped shoulders and bowed head, I grabbed my hat and walked in the direction of the trail the horse had taken to bring me into the meadow. I walked past it and began a gradual climb that led to a small meadow. Two elk cows looked at me as I moved to the edge of the meadow. I chuckled to myself.

"I wonder what they are thinking?" I said partially out loud. "My guess is they have never seen a naked man before."

I could see the darkening of the sky as I looked up the ridge in front of me. Still I kept walking, and soon I saw a snowflake, then another. Suddenly the sky was filled with little white flakes. I kept walking uphill, following a deer trail barely visible through the snow. I smelled the strong scent of bull urine close by and looked down to see steam rising off the moist ground where a bull had marked his territory. They were beginning to rut and I instinctively knew that he was not very far away.

A blast of arctic air hit me square in the face and chilled my body. Reluctantly I turned around and started back in the direction I had come. The snow fell harder and it was impossible to follow the trail. Still I moved, feeling the cold air on my naked skin. I pulled my hat down further on my head and tightened its string. Finally I came out into my meadow, which was by this time covered in snow. The blue spruce and the sleeping bag looked awfully good to me and I crawled in, pulled the canvas cover over my head, and fell fast asleep.

Chapter 2

"The beginning is the most important part of the work."

Plato

I WAS AWAKENED before dawn the next morning by the sounds of nearby coyotes. I listened with great interest as they yapped. I estimated that they were just across the draw from me, and from the sound of things there were at least half a dozen.

A squirrel scolded me from just above my head in the spruce. He had been eating and the leavings from his meal were strewn all over my canvas sleeping bag cover.

"Leave me alone," I heard myself say. "I'm not bothering you. Quit bothering me."

A Steller's jay landed on a nearby pine and began to scold me as well.

"Go to hell," I said with resolve as I chunked a small stone in his direction.

I was miserable, and nothing those guys could do would or could change my depression.

"Your attitude sucks!" Now I was talking to myself. "Go to hell. Leave me alone with your positive attitude crap," I heard myself answering.

I chuckled for a second and soon the chuckle turned to tears once again. I grabbed my pad and began to write.

I was giving Ann Meadows a ride on the back of my bicycle when I felt the urge to do something I had never done before. I stopped the bike, turned, and kissed her firmly on the lips.

"What was that for?" she asked.
"I don't know, it just seemed like something I needed to do," I answered.
"Well, I sure wasn't ready for that. Do you think you could do it again?"

I remember that first kiss to this day. And the second was better than the first. I really liked kissing and promised myself right then and there that I would do a lot of it in the future. That was a promise that I have kept all my life.

Grade school was a bit boring for me. I was much more interested in playing football, baseball, or any sport than in learning English or studying history. I was also much more interested in girls. But I did enjoy reading. Miss Bertha had done her job.

In the summers Mother put Ann and me in swimming lessons and I really took to it. I went through every course that Red Cross offered over the next few years and became not just a good swimmer but an excellent swimmer. I also began to learn to dive during those years.

When I found out that Daddy was an Eagle Scout, that was enough for me. I wanted to be one too. As soon as I was eligible I enrolled in Cub Scouts and quickly achieved rank after rank from Wolf to Bear to Lion. We moved from the Beverly area to Rose Hill when I was in the third grade. Mother took Ann and me to Sunday school and church at the Baptist church a couple of blocks from our house. We went to daily vacation Bible school and were well schooled in the Bible and its teaching. I was eight when I accepted Jesus Christ into my life as my personal Savior and was baptized.

Daddy came home about three years later from the sanitarium and was able to start working again. I was eleven at the time and had just started in Boy Scouts and had a paper route throwing the Dallas Morning News. I can remember Mama and Daddy helping me roll those papers every morning while they had their coffee. At age twelve I had two paper routes — the Dallas paper and the Texarkana Gazette. I had one hundred and sixty-three customers on my Gazette route. The cost of the paper was 35 cents per week. I collected 70 cents from each customer every other week. It was a great business experience.

I threw my routes mostly from my bicycle, but Daddy often would drive me, especially if it was bad weather. Mama got up early to go to work, so we were all up at about 5 A.M. They really helped me and encouraged me to be the best I could be.

I was really into scouting by this time and actively going through the ranks of Tenderfoot, Second Class, and First Class. I loved camping and being outdoors. I even loved my first snipe hunt when I was left holding the bag for the elusive snipe for hours. I felt right at home in the woods, even at night. I was a great fire builder and tent setter, but I hated cooking. Other scouts took advantage of that fact and cooked for me, and I usually set up the tents, started the fires, and did the dishes.

I continued to enter and win swim meets on a regular basis. It didn't matter what stroke or what distance — I nearly always won.

"It's at Pete's Service Station, Daddy, and it's only fifty bucks. Will you look at it with me?" I asked.

"Okay, Son, we'll go up after supper. But I really have to think about this one. Twelve is awfully young to own a car."

I talked to both Daddy and Mama till I was blue in the face and finally they gave in and let me buy the prettiest little 1929 Model A two-door you ever saw. It was true that I didn't have my driver's license and couldn't get one until I was fourteen, but I owned a car that I bought with my own money. It felt good. Daddy let me drive it as I threw my papers in the morning, but only if he was riding with me. By the time I got my driver's license at age fourteen I was a great driver and was on my second Model A, a four-door 1931 beauty with leather seats. I paid $250 for that baby. I wish I had it today.

A very significant event occurred in my life in the eighth grade. Football was my passion and I had been playing football in school-issued shoes. My feet hurt so bad I could hardly walk and Daddy took me to a foot doctor.

"You mean his arches fell just like that?" Daddy was asking the podiatrist.

"Just like that. I'm surprised he can walk at all. It has to just kill him."

"Will he have flat feet?"

"I'm afraid so. For the rest of his life."

"Well, what can we do for him now?" Daddy asked.

"We have to get him in some supportive shoes with laces. We will need to build up those shoes with wedges to keep him walking."

That was just what I wanted to hear. Everyone was wearing penny loafers and he was going to put me in built-up, lace-up shoes. I don't think so. But it happened just that way. I still tried to play football, but the pain was so agonizing that I could just hardly do it at all.

A bull elk bugled not too far from my seat under the spruce. I looked for him for a couple of minutes, then stood up and moved from under the spruce.

I hadn't eaten for three days but was not in the least bit hungry. It's funny how your body can do without food for so long. Water is the important ingredient. As long as a person has water they can survive for an extended period of time without food, well over a month.

Carrying my journal, I moved down the slope toward the creek. I moved slowly, hoping to get a look at the bull. My tears clouded my vision and I knew that the likelihood of me being able to see him was slim. As the slope got steeper, my feet slipped and I found myself on my backside again, this time with a little less skin. I stayed where I had fallen and listened to the creek, which was by now only a few feet in front of me. It was peaceful here. I laid my hat on the ground, ran my fingers through my hair, and began to write once again, recounting my teenage years.

Even though I had my paper routes, my summers were spent teaching swimming lessons as a water safety aide at the swimming pool for the American Red Cross. I took my Junior Life Saving test three times and passed it all three times. The first was when I was eleven, once at twelve, then again at thirteen. Finally the Red Cross made an age exception and gave me the badge.

I continued my scouting and advanced through the rank of Star, then Life. I began working on the God and Country Award, completing one year of service with the First Baptist Church to complete that award.

That was an interesting time in my life. Dr. James Coggin was our pastor, and he and I became close friends during this time. I can remember one very interesting conversation that had an impact on my life.

"Dr. Coggin, I need to ask you your opinion on something that has been bothering me," I said one day.

"What is it, Jake?"

"It's about dancing. I hear from others that Baptists don't believe in dancing. Is that true?"

"That is an interesting question. The Baptist doctrine doesn't specifically say 'Thou shalt not dance.' Basically we believe that anything that causes a person to stray from the teachings of Jesus Christ should be discarded from our lives. Dancing is one of those things that each person has to address for himself. For example, let me ask you this question. When you dance with a girl, does it in any way make you feel sexual toward that girl?"

"I just love to dance. Fast... slow. It doesn't matter to me. When I hear the music I just want to get up and dance. I even dance when there is no music. I just love to dance. Sexual thoughts. Wow, that's heavy. To be honest with you, I can just look at a girl and have those kinds of thoughts. When I dance I just seem to flow with everything that is around me. It makes me feel good to dance."

"Jake, for you there is no reason I can see for you not to dance because you dance for the right reasons. Go and dance and don't worry about those people who believe it is wrong. It can be wrong for some people. I can see that it is not wrong for you. If you can dance when there is no music... when things are not going your way... in times of despair, you will always be happy. Dancing is a way to celebrate life. Celebrate."

While I'm on the subject of church, my parents always took me to Sunday school and church. Even when Daddy was in the sanitarium, Mama took Ann and me every Sunday except when we stayed in Shreveport over a Sunday. After Daddy came home from the sanitarium, we really began to go to church. There was Sunday school, church, Training Union, church, Wednesday night choir practice, and church. Daddy said he made a deal with Jesus before one of his operations and he definitely lived up to his end of the bargain, which was to work in and for Christianity with every ounce of strength he possessed. He became Chairman of the Board of Deacons of the First Baptist Church and spent all of his waking hours working on projects of a Christian nature.

He and Mama tithed much more than most. I remember a time when the IRS challenged them on their donations. The agent just could not believe that anyone would give so much away when they made so little. He was astonished to see all the records of their donations to others, and before long he was going to our church. My parents had an impact on everyone.

Daddy set up rescue missions and passed out Gideon Bibles. He was always available to help someone in need.

We never had much in the way of material wealth, but we had love in our tiny little house. There was plenty of that to go around.

I stopped writing for a minute and looked skyward. My hardworking parents had taught me so much by example.

My daddy suffered a heart attack in March of 1982 and was in intensive care. My mother, sister, and I had limited visits with him and could only visit one at a time. I remember one such visit with my daddy.

"Son, I am so proud of you. No man could be prouder of his son than I am. Do you remember when you bought that bicycle when you were seven?"

"I'll never forget that experience. You showed me the way to get what I wanted. It was easy when I had the path laid out for me."

"It wasn't easy, son, and I know that. You had a difficult childhood with me sick and all."

"I had a great childhood, Daddy. I did everything I wanted to do and had everything I wanted. You taught me that I could have anything, that the world is mine for the taking," I said reflectively.

"Mama and I never had much to give you and Ann."

"That's certainly not true. You gave us everything. You gave us love. What else is there?" I countered.

"I need you to be aware of one more thing. You are probably already aware of it, but I want to point it out to you anyway." He was struggling a little to speak. *"Son, the only thing we really have in this world is our own self-confidence. That's it. There is really nothing else. God gives us the ability to reason for ourselves, but he lets us make the choices in our lives. If we live by our values and stay true to ourselves, we develop self-confidence. If we don't, we lose it. A man without self-confidence is a man lost to himself, and a man lost to himself is lost to the world.*

*You have to like yourself... no... you have to love
yourself to have self-confidence. God created us
in his own image. How can we not love
ourselves?*

*"You have a lot of confidence, Son. It is your
power, your way to a happy life. Stay true to
yourself, no matter what obstacles you find
yourself facing, and you will have a wonderful
journey through this life."*

*Daddy's voice trailed off then and he fell into a
deep relaxed sleep.*

That conversation had a major impact on my life. As I thought about it more, I understood what he was saying. He had helped me gain self-confidence at age seven.

The thoughts of Daddy put me into a reflective mood and I thought of Mama, remembering the four difficult years she spent without Daddy after his passing. It had been a long siege for her, and Alzheimer's is a cruel way to live. Before the second heart attack took Daddy's life, he had called me into his hospital room.

"Son, you have got to take care of Mama," he said. "She can't take care of herself."

"Sure, Daddy, but you will have plenty of time to take care of her yourself. You are going to be alright."

"Son, this is it. My time is up. It is time for me to go," he said.

Being the eternal optimist, I had left Texarkana to go back to my home in Las Colinas. The call came later that night. Daddy had a second heart attack on March 23, 1982. One he did not survive.

Once again I began to sob, and for about an hour I laid across the boulder, crying like a baby. I had never cried until my daddy died... never. I was too tough to feel any emotion. Nothing made me cry. Men did not cry, or so I thought. But when my daddy died, I cried and cried and cried. I just could not quit, and from that day forward I allowed myself to cry. My hero was gone, and in his death I had learned another lesson: Real men do cry. Real men feel.

When there were no more tears, I began to write once again.

My daddy was the finest Christian man I have ever met. He will always be my hero. He believed that every person in the world was important, regardless of his or her position in life. The president of a bank was no more important to him than a homeless person. He had love and respect for them all and went way out of his way to help those in need. As I write about Daddy, God rest his sweet soul, I think about what he used to say when people were having problems in their lives.

"Find someone in need and help them," he would say. "There is always someone that you can help and there is always someone worse off than you."

What a great man my father was. Absolutely the greatest man I have ever known. More than that — my father was the greatest man I will ever know.

Tears began to flow once again. I was in memory mode. Instinctively I felt the presence of both my mama and daddy. Their spirits would help me through my current crisis. I could call on them at any time and they would be there for me.

Man is an interesting animal. We run from pain to pleasure. We just don't want to feel pain so we try to block it out of our lives. We feel pain and we drink alcohol. We feel pain and we blame everyone but ourselves. We feel pain and we take drugs to block it. Pain is nature's way of telling us something is wrong. We have to listen to our bodies. We have to feel our pain and determine its cause if we are to correct it. I planned to embrace the pain I was in, determine its cause, and look for the solution to correct it.

What great parents. What a great legacy they had left. I had been so fortunate. My mother never complained. Never. She just went about her business and played the hand she had been dealt. Daddy's terrible disease didn't slow her down one bit. She just continued to work. Mama was all about sacrifice. She was the sole breadwinner for many years. She was very smart, effective, and a wonderful mother. Her death after a lengthy bout with Alzheimer's had almost been a blessing.

I had burned up the highways between Dallas and Texarkana after Daddy's death checking on her. I could tell she wasn't the same, but it never dawned on me that Daddy had kept her dementia from Ann and me. Looking back on it, the signs were there. One Thanksgiving she put a turkey in the oven and forgot to turn the oven on. She said the oven was broken. Daddy said he would get it fixed.

She was my mother and I just always saw her as smart, capable, and ready to do anything for her family. It was difficult for me to accept the fact that she was anything but perfect. I noted that she was having trouble with her checkbooks, so I helped her with that. Being the eternal optimist, I knew that she was just grieving for Daddy.

My sister lived in Independence, Kentucky, at the time. It was difficult for her to see Mama at all, so I took it upon myself to help her. I bought her a puppy so that she would have something to love — that was a big mistake.

The neighbors helped me understand that Mama was no longer capable of taking care of herself. She was dangerous in the car and had no business driving. It broke my heart to make the tough decisions that led to taking away her freedom. I had to sell her car, then her home. Those were the hardest decisions I ever had to make. I moved her to Dallas where I could be near her.

I placed her in a beautiful assisted-care facility near my home. She had her own apartment, furnished with her own furniture along with some new pieces. She had plenty to do and I saw her every day, and for a while she seemed to be getting along just fine. I would take her to my home in Las Colinas often for dinner and she and I would have lunch together about twice a week. One day I received an alarming phone call from the manager of the place where she was living.

"Jake, we had an incident with your mother this morning. She got after one of our employees with a knife. You will have to find another place for her to live."

I was in total denial about my mother's condition. Because I was so convinced that her condition stemmed from grieving for my father, I found a place in Dallas where she could live with a trained psychologist. I just knew that this lady would be able to help get her through the grieving and soon I would have my old mama back.

It did not work that way. Soon she was living with us in our house. There she would spend hours talking to the mirror. Her reflection she viewed as her sister. I gradually accepted that my mama was no longer the person I had known for so many years. I learned to laugh to keep from crying like the one time my daughter, Jamie, was introducing me to her date for the evening. We were in the playroom, which was covered with mirrors.

"Daddy, this is Mike. Mike, my father, Jake," Jamie said, making the introduction.

"Nice to meet you, Mike. And this is my mother," I said as I introduced him to my mother who was standing close to the full-length mirror at the end of the room.

"Nice to meet you, Mike. And this is my sister, Dee," she said, pointing to her own reflection in the mirror.

The look on that poor boy's face was totally priceless. We had to laugh about it to keep from crying. Not long after that, Mama became incontinent. I had to place her in a nursing home near my home. My sister had moved to Austin, but had a difficult time watching Mother progressively get worse. I recommended she stay away. "I just can't deal with it," she said. I understood.

I visited Mama every day, in the morning and evening. Sometimes they were short visits — just checking in. Early on the morning of July 6, 1986, I had planned to just check in on her and be on my way. I had a full day planned and I needed to be about my business. I felt something strange as I walked in her room that morning. Something was different. I looked at her tired old face, hugged her close to me, and said as I always said, "Good morning, Mama. And how are you this fine morning?"

She opened her eyes then and looked into mine. Those beautiful, tired old eyes were saying something. Her soul was talking to my soul. She opened her mouth and tried to speak, and I leaned closer to her, placing my ear close to her mouth. It had been months since she had been able to say anything. She tried so hard that day. She tried again, but nothing came out. I could see the frustration in her eyes and I instinctively knew what she was trying to say to me.

I held her close and whispered in her ear, "I know, Mama, and it's okay. I know you are ready, and it's okay. You will get to see Daddy again. I know you love me, Mama. And you know I love you too. It's okay, Mama."

She looked up at me one more time. Her eyes spoke volumes. Then she fell into a deep, peaceful sleep. I stayed there holding her hand for hours, just watching her sleep. Finally I left. Later that day I received the call.

Mama had gone to be with Daddy.

Chapter 3

"One of the first conditions of happiness is that the link between Man and Nature shall not be broken."

Leo Tolstoy

AFTER MY TEARS SUBSIDED I grabbed my hat, scooted down the creek bank, and stepped into the cold water. I laughed as I felt the sun bathing my body with its warmth.

"Cold water on my feet... hot sun on my skin. On average I guess I am just about perfect," I thought.

I found a boulder right in the middle of the fast-moving current, placed my journal on it, and began to take a bath. I gasped for air as I scooped the water into my hair and it ran down my back. There is nothing quite as refreshing as taking a bath in a mountain stream. It was cold.

I crawled up on the boulder to air dry in the rays of the warm sun and felt much better. After I had dried, I stretched out to soak up the sun, then once again I put my pen to the paper.

I loved being a Boy Scout. Most of all I loved the camping trips into the forest. Camp Preston Hunt was our camp, which was about ten miles from Texarkana on the Arkansas side. Our scoutmaster in Troop 7 was James Bennett, who was a cancer survivor. He loved to tell us the scariest ghost stories about ax murderers and such at night. Then he would laugh and go to sleep while most of us kept a vigil throughout the night watching for the murderer. I loved being scared. Mostly I loved overcoming my fear. Scouting was very important to me.

I stood at attention and began to recite the Scout Oath aloud.

"On my honor, I will do my best to do my duty to God and my country and to obey the Scout Law, to help other people at all times, to keep myself physically fit, mentally awake, and morally straight."

I thought about the Scout Slogan and the Scout Law, and began to recite them aloud.

"Do a good turn daily," I said, remembering the slogan that had been mine for as long as I could remember.

Then I began to quote the Scout Law that had been such an important part of my life. "A Scout is trustworthy, loyal, helpful, friendly, courteous, kind, obedient, cheerful, thrifty, brave, clean, and reverent."

I sat back down on the boulder and once again began to write.

Not that I was a perfect young man. I wasn't, and I got into as much mischief as any young man. My biggest problem, it seemed, was because I liked girls a lot. Maybe it wasn't a big problem, but girls seemed to be constantly on my mind. I guess most of the boys my age were thinking along the same lines. We all had raging hormones. I devoted a lot of time to the pursuit of girls. I loved everything about them. I loved the way they walked and the way they talked. I loved what they wore. I loved to be with them. I especially loved to kiss them.

The difference in my life to that of other boys my age was that I worked nearly all the time in one job

*or another, and when I wasn't working I was doing
something with scouting or church. Church and choir
proved to be a wonderful place to spend time with the
opposite sex. I was in the Junior Church Choir, which
was filled with beautiful girls. We took a lot of
church-sponsored trips to sing at different places, and
I was always finding a way to sit at the back of the
bus with some real cute girl and neck all the way to
and from the designated place we were to sing.*

*Our choir director caught me one time and at the
next group meeting said, "It has come to my attention
that there has been some courting in the back of the
bus. We will not tolerate this kind of behavior at all.
Do I make myself clear?"*

*He looked straight at me as he asked the question.
I, of course, said yes and made myself a promise to be
more careful in the future.*

*They call the years when one goes through puberty
the "confusion" years. I was never very confused in
those years, and some of my best memories come from
those years. I had my paper routes and became the
"Carrier of the Month" and in the summer I taught
swimming. I spent one summer at Camp Pioneer in
Mena, Arkansas, as a Boy Scout counselor in charge of
canoeing. I was also inducted into the Order of the
Arrow and became a regular on the Indian Dance
Team.*

*The Order of the Arrow is Scouting's national
honor society and it recognizes scouts who best exem-
plify the Scout Oath and Law in their daily lives. To
become a member was exciting for me. I'll never forget
the induction ceremony for the Order of the Arrow.
Since I was a counselor, the tapping out ceremony was
much harder on me than any of the other inductees.
Each inductee had to spend the night alone in the
woods. We were blindfolded, a cedar wreath was*

placed on our brows, and we were led into the woods
and left to find our way back to camp.

Because I was a counselor and a versatile woodsman, the group took me to the famous "haunted
house" where an ax murderer had supposedly killed
five people. He was also supposed to haunt the house
on a regular basis.

The house was legendary in scouting circles. I was
left in that house and was supposed to count to 1000
before I took off my blindfold. Then I was to build a
fire and burn the wreath around my forehead. Need-
less to say, I was very apprehensive. I didn't want any
part of that house. By the time I had counted to 1000
my mind was made up. I was going to distance myself
from that house as quickly as possible. Without benefit
of a flashlight I probably was two miles from that
place when I finally made my fire.

I always had a job. One summer I cut hay and
hauled it even though I inherited "hay fever" from my
mother. I would throw a bale and sneeze, throw a
bale and sneeze, but I stayed with it until the job was
over. My pay was 50 cents per hour. Those were fun
years. I was reminded of those years at a class
reunion when Jimmy Jones brought a movie of me
popping the head off a six-foot chicken snake.

Daddy signed a hardship paper for me and I took
my driver's test in the Model A when I was fourteen. I
passed with ease. I had been driving with my parents
in the car for the better part of two years. Now I could
drive anywhere I wanted anytime I wanted. It was a
big deal for a fourteen-year-old to have a car. It certainly improved my status with the opposite sex. Mostly
only older boys had cars. I had one of the few sets of
wheels in junior high.

The Model A was great, but it wasn't exactly a girl
magnet. What could I do? I traded the perfectly

wonderful Model A four-door sedan for a 1948 Ford convertible. Now I had all the girls. They all wanted to go riding with me. The top was always down and I drove along with sometimes as many as ten girls in my car, which eventually caused the Ford to blow a head gasket. Oh well, it was only money. Besides, it's hard to know which girl you want to zero in on when you have so many in your car; a problem not easily solved.

About this time, I started working for Piggly Wiggly Food Stores on weekends. I still had my paper routes but began my career as a "sack" boy and stock clerk. Later that same year I was accidentally locked in the produce freezer just as the store was closing. I was absolutely scared to death and never got over my fear of being in tight places. I am still a bit claustrophobic today, although I have worked on it through scuba diving.

An active young man learns a lot during puberty. One of the Piggly Wiggly ladies I worked with had a sister from out of town who spent some time teaching me some things that I was only too eager to learn at that time of my life. She was sixteen and I was fourteen. She was an exceptional teacher and I was eager to learn. I was a great student.

Without question I was an admirer of the opposite sex; from the clothes they wore to the way they moved to the scent of their hair. I was totally enamored with them. Now, after this latest encounter, I found I loved their parts.

At fourteen I became an Eagle Scout. It was quite an accomplishment to achieve the rank of Eagle, and I have always felt it to be one of my greatest life accomplishments. Shortly thereafter I became an Explorer Scout and joined Sea Scout Ship 29. I worked diligently on all the Explorer ratings with a passion

and became the proud holder of the coveted Explorer
Silver Award. I knew of no other scout to have three
"dangly" medals on his pocket. Eagle Scout, God and
Country Award, and the Explorer Silver Award hung
on my pocket.

It's no wonder I was selected to represent the Caddo
Area Council of the Boy Scouts of America and make
the report to the governor. I also served as an Emergency Service Explorer and was actively involved with
search and rescue missions throughout the four-state
area. I learned scuba diving and served as one of two
divers that would dive for victims who had drowned. I
never found a dead person under water, and for that
I was eternally grateful. The thought of having a body
come into view in murky water used to haunt me.

I noticed a movement in the water below and glanced in that direction. Two brook trout moved from the swift water into the still water
below the boulder on which I sat. As I continued to watch, they
seemed to remain completely motionless in the clear water. Feeling a
slight chill, I glanced skyward. The warm sun was now replaced with
an ominous dark cloud.

"Storm clouds are building," I thought.

I was on a roll and my pen was flying over the pages in my spiral
notebook. I knew that to get where I wanted to go I had to know
where I was. Instinctively, I knew that where I was in my life had
everything to do with where I had been. It seemed a simple formula to
me. If a person is lost, that person needs to stop and try to figure out
where he is. Recounting where one has been seems to be the step
that gets a person to where he is. If a lost person continues on aim-
lessly, he will continue to stay lost and may never be found. In rescue
work we continually looked for people who never took the time to just
stop and try to figure out where they were. They continued on aim-
lessly, hoping to find their way.

I was lost. I was not lost in the San Juans. Just because I didn't
know where I was, I wasn't lost. I was right at home there. I was lost

in the sense that I had lost my way in my life. I wanted to find me. I wanted to be comfortable in my own hat. Mine. No other hat. Just mine. Daddy had always told me that all the answers to all the questions were inside of me. I just had to ask the right question and the answer would come. He always stressed asking specific questions. Focus on what you want to know.

He often quoted from the Bible, "Ask and it shall be given unto you. Seek and ye shall find."

I would find my answers. Once I knew where I had been, I felt I could, once again, get on the trail to lead me to where I wanted to go. I grabbed for the ballpoint.

I have never quite understood the drive that moved me to try to do things others could not or would not do. Maybe it was because I knew I could do them. Maybe it was the message of the book The Little Engine That Could that caused my determination. I really do not know. Maybe it was because of what my daddy taught me when he told me I could have a bicycle if I really wanted it. I just seemed to always want to try something I wasn't supposed to do at an age when I wasn't supposed to be able to do it. I loved a challenge. If I were challenged to do something I would give it my best shot.

At age thirteen I wanted to learn to be a springboard diver. I was pretty clumsy, as most boys are at that age. I would watch others do an intricate dive and then I would attempt to do it. It didn't matter that I would hit wrong or that blood would come out of my ears; I just kept trying. Texarkana had neither a swimming nor diving team. Bud Sower, however, seemed to know a lot about diving and I asked him to help me. He told me to visualize every part of the dive, from the time I walked onto the diving board until I hit the water. I was to do this over and over until I could see myself doing the dive right. Then I should try it.

He worked with me a couple of times and then told my daddy that I would never make a diver. According to him I was far too big and far too clumsy. His statement inspired me.

"Puff, puff, chug, chug... I think I can—I think I can—I think I can..."

I continued to practice physically and mentally as well. The visualization became an important part of my diving and began to creep into my swimming as well. Before attempting a dive I would see my steps, my hurdle, my body doing what it was supposed to do, and then the perfect entry. That technique helped me tremendously. In swimming I would visualize how good it felt to be in the water, how the flip turn would feel, and how it felt to get the medal for first. It worked.

Bud didn't think I was so clumsy about three years later when I won springboard diving championships all over the East Texas and Arkansas area. He wanted to coach me then. I felt he wanted to take credit for teaching me to dive. I do give him the credit for inspiring me to learn to dive on my own. Most of all, the visualization technique he described to me has made a profound difference in every part of my life.

It seemed my life was always about proving myself. To whom? For what purpose? Would I ever just be content? I had none of the answers, only the questions. Still, I knew that one part of my life just craved an adventure. One part just could not be satisfied with the status quo. One part demanded to be challenged. It demanded adventure. The harder and tougher, the better.

In high school I loved several things. I loved sports. I loved cars. I loved girls. I loved challenging myself. I received my Senior Life Saving certificate at age fourteen and I became a lifeguard and continued to teach swimming for the Red Cross. The Red Cross sent me to National Aquatic School when I was sixteen. The requirement age was eighteen. A college cheerleader and I became more than just friends at the school. She was three years my senior.

I was the best swimmer at the aquatic school and received both the Red Cross Water Safety Instructor rating and the First Aid Instructor rating. Back in Texarkana I became a specialist in teaching Junior and Senior Life Saving. I was tough but the people I taught knew what to do in an emergency.

My high school years were great. My favorite subject was drama, and I was fortunate enough to land a lead in both the junior and senior plays and in a series of one-act plays that we did later.

When my arches had fallen in junior high and my football days came to an end, I felt I had lost everything. Because I identified myself as a football player, I thought my world had come to an end. Now, I was an outsider who loved the game. My feet and ankles would not allow me to play. Still, I wanted to be a part of the team. I wanted to help score touchdowns.

By popular vote I was elected cheerleader at Texas Senior High. Now I could offer my help to our team. Now I could be a part once again. Also by popular vote, I was fortunate enough to win the Best Personality Award, an honor of which I was very proud.

All through junior high and high school I had a job, somewhere. I was a paper boy. At Piggly Wiggly I was a sack boy and stock clerk. At Boyds Tool House I cleaned tools and stocked the warehouse. At the S&H

Green Stamp Store I was a stock boy. At Collin & Williams I started as a delivery boy and ended up selling exclusive men's clothes. It was at Collins & Williams that I bought my first good suit of clothes.

Most of my money I invested either in cars or into a registered Black Angus Beef herd that I raised on a little farm Daddy owned in Redwater, Texas. I planned to use that herd to get my college education paid for. I remember so well the day I had to call the sheriff out to the farm to look at two of my registered Angus cows that had been shot.

"It was poachers that done it," he said emphatically. "They drive down these roads at night and use a high beam light. They think they are shooting deer, I imagine."

"Do you think you will catch them?" I asked.

"I doubt it. We will patrol this road a little more often. I'll file a report with the game warden too. He will be interested in what is going on here."

I was sick. Those cows had cost me $200 each and that was in 1957. Working full time in the summer I made about $160 per month, so my summer wages had been for nothing. It had taken just two shots from a high-powered rifle for my dreams to be shattered.

"Shoot my cows. Shoot my college education. All that work for free… all my dreams. Somebody ought to shoot you. And I'm just the man to do it," I screamed in disgust.

Part of the problem was that the cows were springing heavy. When the poachers shot the cows, they killed the calves too — calves that I planned to sell when they were older. The proceeds would go into my bank account for college.

Hardly a month later I found my prize heifer dead in the pasture, partially eaten and with suspicious-looking tracks all around. I called the game warden for Bowie County.

"You are as right as you can be," he said. "It was a pack of wolves. They have been all around these parts and we have a government trapper in the county now. I'll send him over here and maybe he can trap them. Meantime, we are paying a bounty on those things. They are killing livestock all over the county. Just bring in their ears and you can collect a $15.00 bounty."

"What can I get for the ears of the poachers that shot my cows?" I asked.

"Wish I could give you a bounty on those guys too. Sure would like to catch them."

"Me too," I said.

Since that time I have found it difficult to be very excited about those who want wolves to return to the ecosystem in the United States. I'm convinced had they walked in my shoes and seen their prize heifer ripped apart by a group of the most deadly killers in the world they might feel a little differently. It is easy to watch them on TV and say, "We need to bring the wolves back." It's entirely different when one works all summer to see his prize heifer's neck ripped open and the insides strewn all over the place — and maybe see a college education ruined — by a pack of wolves. Maybe if they had to work for a living they would know.

The government trapper caught some of the pack and I killed a couple with my .30-.30. I found myself wishing I could shoot the poachers too.

In high school, cars were my passion and I had bought and paid for nine cars by the time I graduated high school. My best memories come from a 1953 Chevrolet convertible. That baby was a girl magnet.

I opted for Texarkana Junior College my first two years where I was a cheerleader and was elected as a fraternity vice president. It was at Texarkana College that I began to date a girl who seemingly was uninterested in me. She was beautiful and her name was Jackie Wilkins. Her lack of interest was a total challenge.

Chapter 4

"Every day you make progress. Every step may
be fruitful. Yet there will stretch out before you
an ever-lengthening, ever-ascending, ever-
improving path. You know you will never get to
the end of the journey. But this, so far from
discouraging, only adds to the joy and glory of
the climb."

Sir Winston Churchill

BEING LOST came to my mind once again and I remembered
how as an Emergency Service Explorer and serving on the Rescue
Squad in Bowie County, we had looked for people who were lost. The
lost three-year-old came to mind. We found him dead, face down in a
creek. I will never forget the anguish on that young mother's face as
she grieved over her son.

Being lost at three is one thing. Being lost in your forties is still
another. I knew what I had to do, so I started once again in my journal.

*After two years at Texarkana College I transferred
to Texas A&M to major in animal husbandry. I continued competing in swimming and diving events
throughout the region and put on diving exhibitions
on a regular basis. Texas A&M's swimming coach, Art
Adamson, saw me warming up in the swimming pool*

before I was to try out for the diving team there and, after timing me, placed me on the swimming and water polo teams.

"Son, you have a good stroke. Do you mind if I time you?"
"I'm here to try out for the diving team," I said.
"Just let me time you two lengths of the pool."
"Okay," I said.

My first semester at A&M was terrible. I was classified a second-semester sophomore. The adjustment was most difficult. Not only was I adjusting to being away from home, but I also was adjusting to being away from a girl I was trying my best to impress. Jackie was my greatest challenge, since she had only previously dated football players and I was just a lowly swimmer. Not only that, in 1961 A&M was an all-male college. No females, aside from a few wives of Aggies, were on campus.

The dean of students called me into his office after the grades were posted for my first semester there.

"Well, Mr. Billingsley, I don't know what is going on in your life, but I do know this: Your grades have to improve or you are out of this college. You did not make a single F this semester but D's are not going to cut it at this school. Now, understand me completely. If your grades do not improve next semester considerably, you will no longer be a student here."
"Yes, sir. I will do better next semester."
"I hope so, Mr. Billingsley. I surely hope so."

I knew what my problem was. I needed to be near my woman, so I nervously proposed to Jackie. What surprised me most was that she said yes. At age *nineteen, and at semester's end, Jackie, the girl who seemed totally uninterested in me, and I were married. Living with her settled me down. My grades improved. The next semester the dean called me into his office.*

"Mr. Billingsley," he said, "you went from scholastic probation to Distinguished Student in one semester. I must say I am pleasantly surprised. I really did not expect you to make it. Keep up the good work."
"Yes, sir," I said. "I told you I would do better this semester."
"That you did, Mr. Billingsley, that you did."

I focused on studying from then on and I maintained that Distinguished Student designation the remaining years I was at A&M. While Jackie worked, I went to school, and I also worked for Coach Adamson, managing both the indoor and outdoor pools.

"Funny, the things you do when you're growing up," I thought. "Like the time I decided to drink after finals."
My pen was ready to write about the incident.

After finals my senior year I did a very stupid thing — I decided it was time for me to celebrate by drinking. To that point I had barely tasted alcohol. It was not that I was a prude; it was more that I was a highly conditioned athlete. My father hated the stuff. He had told me tales about when he was a detective and how alcohol had impaired people's judgment. He told me stories of men beating their wives and kids while drunk.
It just never did seem to be something I needed to do. But for some strange reason I decided to drink after that final, and I really tied one on, mixing all

kinds of alcohol. I found myself "knee walking" drunk for the first time in my life. I even showed the other partiers how to do a racing dive from the kitchen table to the floor.

I could barely function the next day. Yet, as manager of the large outdoor pool, I had responsibilities. Just hearing barefoot footsteps on the concrete was too much. Pools are noisy. Kids in pools are really noisy. The only place I could find any respite from the terrible headache was on the bottom of the pool. I took over the vacuuming that day. In fifteen feet of water with the pressure around me, I found some peace. That is, until I breathed. Inhaling was fine, but when I exhaled the bubbles made my head pound. Heck, even my hair follicles hurt. It was terrible. I held my breath as long as I could. It was in the bottom of that pool in the summer between my junior and senior years that I made a lifetime decision: Anything that could cause one to feel that bad was not right for me. It was a good lesson. I have often wondered how others could like alcohol so much when it makes you feel so bad the next day. I had made the choice to drink the alcohol. The consequence was the hangover. I never did it again.

I couldn't help but wonder why people drink in the first place. Some say they like to drink socially. Okay, but what does that mean? Some say they like to drink when they are with their friends. Are their friends that boring that they have to drink to be with them? Maybe they need a whole new set of friends. Some say they like to drink to drown their sorrow. Why not just help someone worse off than they are? Some say they drink because they are unhappy. Okay, whose fault is that? Do something different in your life to make you happy. Some say they drink because they are happy. Great, but how do you feel the next day?

I would be just as happy if alcohol had never been invented. Others don't feel that way. My lesson was learned the hard way, but it was my lesson. My lesson worked for me. I could not judge other people, I could only judge my choices and my consequences.

Another bad choice I made happened when I was seventeen. Some friends offered me some chewing tobacco while we were duck hunting. My day was spent pulling myself up from the floor of the boat to the edge just to throw up. I never tried chewing tobacco again either.

From the direction of the spring I heard wind blowing through the pine and spruce. It was moving downslope and in my direction. The sound became progressively louder. Leaves began to fall slowly at first, then more rapidly. A gust of cold northern wind chilled my naked skin. I could hear my daddy's voice in the wind as it blew through the trees, saying, "Seek and ye shall find." It was as if he were right there with me, whispering the scripture in my ear.

The more I thought about it the clearer it became.

Every choice has a consequence. I'd made a lot of choices in my life. Some good. Some bad. The tobacco and the alcohol were choices. They were bad choices, but the lessons learned from the bad choices were lifelong lessons that were good. Sometimes what is a bad choice at the time serves to give us the best learning experience. We have to take the responsibility for our choices. We have to take the responsibility for our actions. That is a law of living.

Taking responsibility for our actions is, for some, a difficult thing to do. It is much easier to blame someone or something else for our shortcomings and bad choices. People do it all the time. "I'm this way because..." is an excuse. It is a complete cop-out. If we are to grow in life, we must take responsibility for our choices, both good and bad.

I remembered another example of choice as I wrote.

I was nineteen and at an airfield in Arkansas. Jackie's brother-in-law, Shelton Eakin, was a Gunnery Sergeant in the Marine Corps and was also a skydiver.

For some reason I was terribly scared of heights. Anytime I looked down from a high place I always felt I wanted to jump. My heart would flutter and I found it difficult to breathe. Because I was so scared of heights I decided that the best thing for me to do was to jump out of a plane. I wanted to conquer my fear. But it was a little more than that with me. I felt that I could jump without a static line, which would open my chute for me as I exited the aircraft. I figured that I could do a freefall and pull my own ripcord rather than have the static line do it for me.

Shelton Eakin taught me the PLF (parachute landing fall) during the day, but darkness came before I had the opportunity to jump.

> *"I'm jumping anyway," I stated.*
> *"No, you are not. You have to have at least thirty hours to jump at night," was Shelton's reply.*
> *"Yes, I am, and for the record, I'm jumping without a static line."*
> *"You are absolutely crazy."*

I laughed as I remembered the incident as if it were yesterday. I jumped that night without a static line. When I finally landed, on the concrete runway of the abandoned airfield, I broke my fibula. Choices… consequences. What did I learn from that? Mostly that I am stubborn and a little stupid and that I am a risk-taker who sometimes doesn't evaluate his choices very well. I wrote once again.

> *Interestingly enough the choice that I had made to skydive was one choice. The consequence of that was a broken leg. Explaining why I was on crutches led me to another choice.*
> *While interviewing for jobs my senior year, one group in particular wanted me to come to work for them. When I told the United States Secret Service how*

I had broken my leg they became really interested in me. I guess they figured that anyone who would jump out of an airplane at night without a static line on their first jump was their kind of man. How perfect. A man like that would jump in front of a bullet meant for the President any day. They offered me a job.

One choice had a consequence that led to another choice. Our choices have a "snowballing" effect. One choice. One consequence. It just doesn't seem to work that way. Each choice leads to another and another. With each choice we are, in effect, shaping our lives.

I looked up at the sky again, determined to keep an eye on the clouds to the north that seemed to be moving rapidly in my direction. I wanted to write. I needed to write. I needed to find my way. I was lost. One way or another, I was going to find my way back to my path.

I sensed a presence and slowly turned my head upslope to see a spotted fawn running out of the brush about forty yards away. Another followed close behind. I watched as the two ran to and fro on the slope, continuing in my direction. Behind them, their mother appeared ghostlike from a bush. I remained motionless on the boulder in the middle of the creek. Golden aspen leaves were falling all around and onto my naked body. The three deer walked into the creek not ten yards from where I was sitting and I watched as they drank. I could see their reflection in the still water of the pool formed by a log that had fallen into the swift-moving water. I watched them, being careful not to look directly at them. My years of experience as an outdoorsman had taught me to view them through my peripheral vision. The increasingly strong gusts were coming out of the north and the deer were now just west of me. I knew they would not pick up my scent until they were downwind, and I remained motionless on the rock. I continued to remain motionless until the three had walked back up the slope toward my spruce. Only then did I continue to write.

Out of college I went to work as a ranch manager in Mount Vernon, Texas, for a furniture dealer named L.D. Lowry. Jackie and I moved into a lovely home on the ranch. One month into the position Mr. Lowry called me into his office and said he wanted to get rid of the weeds on the ranch. It was being overrun with goat weeds.

"Great," I said. "I know just the chemical that will do the job."

"There is only one way to get rid of those weeds," Lowry said with a scowl. "You have to pull them up."

"Let me get this straight," I said. "Even though there are chemicals out there that will kill the weeds, you think they should be pulled up. You have lots of acres out here. That will take a long time. Wouldn't it be better and faster to use the chemical?"

"You work for me and I want you to pull them up. Start at the old dam," he said.

I left his office really pissed off and not knowing what to do. This was the stupidest thing I had ever heard in my life. I had 160 hours in training from the finest agricultural school in the country and now I was going to go and pull weeds. I hadn't done that since I pulled weeds while working at my summer job between Texarkana Junior College and A&M. At that time I had worked in the Forestry Department at Red River Army Depot and we had to pull weeds out of the slash pine seedling nursery. But that was only once or twice. Now I was expected to pull weeds on some 3,000 acres. Still, I went to it.

I spent exactly thirty minutes pulling those weeds. The more I pulled, the more I was annoyed at myself. All my life I had hated bullies and power players, and here I was being bullied. It didn't sit right with me so

I hopped in the pickup and headed back to Lowry's office.

"Mr. Lowry, you are looking for someone who wears a number five hat and a size 48 sport coat. I didn't spend the last four years of my life getting a great education so I can pull weeds. I quit."

I stormed out of his office and slammed the door.
"Now what?" I thought. "Jackie is so happy here. We have a great house. I have just quit my first job. What am I going to tell Jackie?"

The Secret Service made a follow-up call during this time and I thought long and hard about taking a job with them. I thought about that choice again and wondered where I would be if I had taken that opportunity. Instead I took another job. I grabbed my journal once again.

We ended up in Smith County where I became assistant county agricultural agent, in charge of the 4-H program and the Junior Beef Show. I worked continually. Seven days a week. I was on a mission. For what? I never knew. Maybe it was to prove that I was not a failure.

While there we began a program to try to stamp out brucellosis in cattle in Texas. I was a strapping young man with plenty of strength. I went with a veterinarian who was to vaccinate the cattle in our area. I became the "chute." My job was to catch the cattle any way I could and hold them for the vet to do his work. I roped some, bulldogged some, and held others to the side of a board fence. I was kicked, slammed into walls, bruised, and beat up, but I enjoyed every minute of the challenge and we did a lot to stamp out the dreaded "bangs" disease in Smith County.

Some of my 4-H'ers wanted me to teach them how to castrate calves. I set up the appointment and an "old-timer" overheard me setting it up.

"You don't want to castrate them things tomorrow," he said emphatically.

"Why not?"

"The moon's not right. Them calves is liable to bleed to death. You need to wait a couple more days."

Now I had 160 hours in animal science and had even taken some classes in veterinary medicine. I was way too smart for this old man.

"I'll take my chances," I told him.

The next morning I castrated three calves and could barely stop the bleeding. That started me thinking that maybe I didn't know everything and that the moon, which could cause the tide to come in and go out, might have some bearing on nature. Maybe even have some bearing on what our personalities are like. The lesson: Maybe I'm not so smart after all. Maybe I don't know everything. Maybe there are some hidden forces at work about which I have no knowledge. Maybe I should be a little more open-minded about things. Great lesson.

Our county office set up a program that we called the F-1 Heifer program to try to bring better quality cattle to the beef industry. I served on the board of the Smith County Farm and Ranch Club and the Smith County Farm Bureau during this time.

Jackie was pregnant, and in December of 1964 I found myself in the waiting room of Mother Francis Hospital in Tyler.

"I'm 90% sure it will be a boy," Jackie's doctor assured me in the waiting room. "I have predicted thousands of these based on the heartbeat and I'm certain you will have a little boy."

Not that it made a bit of difference to me. I just wanted the baby to be healthy and for Jackie to be okay as well. That particular waiting room had two little signs that would light up right after a delivery. A blue one flashed "It's a boy" or a pink one flashed "It's a girl" so the expectant father would know quickly what sex his baby was. There were several people in the waiting room with me, and I watched the signs light up, one after another.

I was visualizing my son and I hunting and fishing together, playing ball together, and doing all kinds of father/son things together. About two in the morning the sign flashed "It's a girl." I thought, "That's nice, someone else had a little girl."

My son and I were doing lots of stuff together in the outdoors. Then all of a sudden it dawned on me that I was the only person in the room. I tore out to the nurses station and told them that a mistake had been made on the sign. I was having a little boy.

The nurse laughed and went into the delivery room to check on the mistake.

"It's not a mistake," she reported. "You have a little girl."

After a short adjustment period I was passing out cigars all over town. I now was not only a husband, but a father as well. Jamie Lyn became the apple of my eye. I lived for her smile, her hugs, and her enthusiasm for learning.

From 1964 to 1967, Jackie's brother-in-law, Marine Shelton Eakin, and I spent a great deal of time together and became close friends. We camped, worked out, hunted, and scuba dived together. We slept only in our sleeping bags, even when snow covered us. Shelton became my mentor. He was tough, physical, and loved the outdoors as much as I. He had been through SEAL type training, jungle training, and all types of training for his job as a reconnaissance Marine. It was a great time in my life to learn from a highly trained Marine.

"Here's the drill, Jake. I am going to throw your scuba tank in the water, then your regulator, then your mask, and then your fins. Your job is to dive down, put the regulator on the tank, get your mask and flippers on, and swim out to that buoy before you come up. Think you can do it?" Shelton asked.

I was game for anything. I knew the water was twelve feet deep but I just knew that I would be able to do it.

"Of course I can," I said with confidence, even though I was a little apprehensive.

I did it. Water was my domain and I was very comfortable with that task. Others were more difficult for me, but I tried until I completed any tasks that my mentor laid out for me on a daily basis. We ran fifteen miles per day, every day, during one full summer we spent together.

I had been writing as fast as I could, hardly looking up. I took a brief moment to stand and look at the now darkening sky. "It's getting worse," I thought. "And just when I feel like I'm getting somewhere. Now let's see, what was I thinking about here? Oh yeah. The honors that had come my way. And the opportunity to work for Texas Power and Light Company. Now I remember. I better get it down before I forget it or before that storm gets here." I picked up my pen and wrote again.

Honors came my way. So did opportunity. Texas Power and Light Company offered me a job as an agricultural consultant and I took it. During this time I was asked to apply for a job to be personal assistant to the President of Texas A&M. I chose not to proceed on that course. Was that a good choice? I will never know. Had I chosen that direction, what would my life have been like?

"Choices and consequences. Our lives are filled with them," I thought. "Like the time I tried to make a speech. I remember I was so embarrassed. I was asked to speak and I made the choice to do it. But I failed miserably. Everyone was looking at me and I just completely lost my train of thought. I remember so well… like it was yesterday. I was trying to tell a joke and I could feel everyone's eyes on me… watching. They were interested in what I was saying and I completely blew it. I forgot the punch line to the joke and just stood there like a doofus. I shudder just thinking of it. But it turned out to be one of the greatest moments of my life."

I grabbed the journal and began to write.

That embarrassing moment challenged me to become a speaker and I spent a number of years doing just that. Sometimes our failures are the greatest motivators in our lives. From failures we can learn the lesson. I asked my company to send me through the Dale Carnegie course and they did. I learned a lot about self-confidence in that course. I also learned how to be an effective speaker. I went through the course a second time as a graduate assistant. Then I began to offer my services as a speaker to various clubs. The more I spoke, the better I became and I honed my skills.

I will forever be indebted to Texas Power and Light for the insight and training they gave me. I will forever remember one of my great teachers within that company. Oran Lewellen taught me how to think and act on my thinking. He taught me that successful people think differently than others. He taught me the principles of setting goals, which I still use today.

He taught me to write down my strengths and my weaknesses each year and to work on items on that list that I wanted to improve. Those items became my objectives and I wrote them down, quantified them, and improved them. He taught me that beliefs should be continually challenged and, if needed, could be changed. He helped me understand my values by asking me to write down what was important in my life.

"Lew," as I called him, started me on a quest for knowledge and understanding that has been ongoing in my life. It has caused me to study all the major religions of the world. Not that I would ever give up Christianity, because I am a Christian, but I felt that studying the religions and the major philosophies would help me become a better person. He introduced me to books like Atlas Shrugged, which made me think. He encouraged me to study, think for myself, and to make my own decisions.

"You give your power away when you allow anyone else to make decisions for you. You are plenty smart enough to make your own decisions. Use study to help you make decisions, but use your intuition after you have all the facts. Your higher self will always guide you in the right direction," he used to say.

Before I moved from Tyler, one of my really good friends in the company was set for retirement. He was as dedicated as I was in his work and seemingly worked all the time including Saturdays and Sundays. He was excited about his retirement and told all of us he planned to fish and play golf after he retired. Two weeks before his retirement party, he died of a stress-related heart attack. I was crushed but I learned very valuable lessons that will stick with me the rest of my life. Those lessons include never putting off those things you want to do in your life. Life is short. Working all the time is fruitless and unfulfilling. Take the time to do the things you want to do. Live each day as if it were your last.

Stephen Levine, an American Spiritual teacher and author, put it this way: "If you were going to die soon and had only one phone call you could make, who would you call and what would you say? And why are you waiting?"

Chapter 5

"Far better it is to dare mighty things, to win
glorious triumphs, even though checkered by
failure, than to take rank with those poor
spirits who neither enjoy much nor suffer
much, because they live in the grey twilight that
knows not victory nor defeat."

Theodore Roosevelt

WRITING IN THE JOURNAL was helping. I could feel that. It always made me feel better to write. Words have so much power. They can motivate or anger. They can cause a person to feel better or worse. Mostly though, I have found by writing things down I would get a firmer grasp on what I was trying to accomplish. In this case I was writing to accomplish a better understanding of myself. I continued.

When an agricultural consultant is getting headlines all over the nation as a speaker, the higher-ups in the company begin to take notice. The headlines sometimes called me a TP&L executive. Heck, I was just a consultant to farmers. Soon I was offered a job in Dallas in the industrial development division, and from there to operations where I reported to the vice president of operations.

The people who had known me as Jake now called me Mr. Billingsley. I did not like it and told them to just call me Jake. It didn't work; they continued to call me Mr. Billingsley.

"I don't like it one bit," I told Lewellen. "My name is Jake, not Mister."

Lew laughed. "When you elevate in a company such as this one to a certain status, everyone calls you Mr. It is a sign of respect. No reason to be upset."

"Well, Lew, people should respect Jake for who he is, not the title he has in the company. I don't like it. My name is Jake and that's what I want to be called."

"Just keep in mind, Jake, that some will feel uncomfortable calling you Jake with your current status. Respect them as well," Lew counseled.

I continued to speak and became known as an after-dinner humorist and motivational speaker. The problem was, it was interfering with my family life, as I was working one job and "moonlighting" with my speaking. I quit the circuit to devote more time to my family. I continued as a speaker locally, however, and continued as president of the Dallas Downtowners Toastmasters Club.

I was asked, for the second time in my life, to consider running for political office such as State Representative, or even Congress. The first time it was suggested was when I was in Tyler. I respectfully declined both times. It was just another choice in my life... and another decision. I was then asked to help candidates learn to speak, and I was more than willing to help them by giving them pointers.

Becoming a good speaker takes much more than a few pointers. It takes a person who is dedicated to *helping his or her audience. The speaker has to be genuine and feel he or she has a message that will be of benefit. Basically, a speaker has to love and relate to the people. The best speakers feel the needs of the audience and find a way to get the message across.*

I tried to teach that the best speakers used stories and anecdotes to get their points across. Jesus did that and he was the greatest of them all.

It was also during this time that I was taught a course called Management by Objectives. It became a part of my life and I was asked to assist in teaching these skills to others in our company. Soon I was traveling and teaching Management by Objectives throughout our fifty-two-county service area.

I liked the program, and the teachings became a part of my daily life. Very simply the program teaches that to know where you want to go, you first have to know where you are. It's kind of like taking a trip. You have to know the location from which you are starting. It is really that simple and that basic, but the course changed my life completely.

A person, group, or company starts by analyzing where he/she/they are in their lives. What are the strengths? What are the weaknesses? It was the same stuff Lewellen had taught me a couple of years before. This is the starting point. We must write down these strengths and weaknesses so we can understand what we need to work on.

Armed with this information, a decision is made as to "where we want to go" — a simple decision but one that can have a profound impact on our lives. Now, we have an objective. We must write it down.

The next step is to determine "how we will get there." There are a lot of ways to reach an objective. There are a lot of directions we can take. When we know where we are and where we want to go and we know our direction of travel, we can make other decisions.

There is nothing difficult or complicated about the concept. It is simple, but it requires thought and a willingness to follow the principles. Often I hear others try to make it difficult. Some teachers act as if they know a secret no one else knows. They use language that is not easy to understand so that they will feel good about themselves. It makes them feel important to present the material in such a fashion as to make them the absolute expert... the guru. Okay, but who are you helping?

Daddy always said, "There is nothing new under the sun."

On and on the simple Management by Objectives thread weaves throughout our lives if we let it. By writing each step down it allows us to quantify our objectives, change our beliefs, and move on, with direction.

I put down my pen for a minute and took a deep breath, feeling the clean fresh mountain air penetrate my lungs. I was on a roll as I wrote. I knew I was getting somewhere with this writing. Where I was going with it I had no earthly idea. Usually I wrote objectives. Now I was writing just to put down on paper some of the more significant events that had an impact on my life. What had shaped my life? I was very much in a self-discovery mode. I began to write once again.

On July 23, 1967, my son, Jay, was born in Irving, Texas. I was totally blessed. I had a beautiful wife and daughter and now I had a son. How blessed could one man be? I just knew that he and I would do everything together. Two outdoorsmen taking on the elements. I was a proud and protective father who would do anything for my family.

It was about this time that TP&L sent its entire top management people through a battery of tests that was followed by a consultation from a noted psycholo-gist. After the tests I went to his office.

Before I could even shake his hand or sit down he said, "What are you doing in manage-ment? You are a salesman and the most natural salesman I have ever tested."

I was still standing at the time.

I answered him by saying, "I'm good at it. I'm good in management."
"Son, you'd be good at anything. You have more drive and determination than any person I have ever tested, and I have been doing this for thirty years. But you are best suited to be in sales. Again, I repeat, you are the most natural salesman I have ever met."

Then he offered me a seat and we had a long dis-cussion on what the tests had shown him. He warned me, "If you don't slow down, you will be dead by the time you are thirty."

I chewed on my ballpoint for a second, remembering the incident.
When the student is ready, the teacher appears. The teacher was right in front of me. He was teaching and I was listening. It was time for a job change.
An objective I had set while in college began to reappear. That objective was to be a millionaire by the time I was thirty. What sales vehicle would take me to that objective? I began reading books on building wealth and the wealthy. It appeared to me that the only sources of true wealth were oil and gas or real estate. I chose real estate.
I began to write once again.

TP&L tried to get me to stay, suggesting that I was being groomed for one of the senior officer positions, but I was determined that my best choice was to move into the field of commercial real estate. I was offered positions by several major commercial real estate companies but chose The Campbell Company because the owner, Bill Campbell, was the only one who turned me down. I was determined that his company was where I should be. It happened. I launched my real estate career. Bill was an excellent teacher and taught me about value. As a result I began to build my net worth. I loved the challenge of making a deal that seemed impossible. The commissions were good and a person was rewarded for his own efforts. The more one worked, the more one would get paid.

It was a tough business. Early on a client of mine cut me right out of a deal.

"Riley, what's going on here?" I asked. "You know I showed you that deal." I wanted some answers.

"You did, Jake. It's nothing personal. It's about business. I'd screw my own grandmother for $20,000."

My thoughts shifted once again back to Shelton Eakin and the times we had spent together.

By this time, Shelton had won the Peacetime Medal for Heroism by saving another Marine's life in a night parachute mission. For that, Gunnery Sergeant Eakin was given special duty in Washington, D.C. He was in charge of the Honorary Color Guard at the nation's capital and was promoted to Second Lieutenant.

While there he volunteered for duty in Vietnam. I asked him why he had taken such a risk.

He explained, "So that my son can walk into a convenience store and buy a Hershey bar or an Almond Joy. In America we enjoy the greatest freedom in the world... the freedom to choose. There are those that would take that freedom from my son. I want to stop them."

I put my friend and mentor Lieutenant Eakin on a plane headed for Vietnam in the late summer of 1967. I knew the man for who he was and what he stood for. I was convinced that this man could single-handedly end that war and I wasn't worried one bit. In fact I watched the news only to try to determine when the North Vietnamese would surrender. This was a real man with real convictions.

One month later, I took Shelton off a plane. This time with an American flag draped across his casket. My best friend had died so that his son might be able to choose between a Hershey bar and an Almond Joy.

Lieutenant Eakin, like countless others, had given his life so that we, in America, might have the greatest single freedom we possess: the freedom to choose. If that freedom is worth dying for, isn't it worth living for?

A single tear rolled down my cheek once again. That had been over twenty years ago and the pain of losing a mentor, a hunting companion, and a best friend was overwhelming. Shelton and I had trained together, swum together, and camped together. We had enjoyed watching a family of raccoons frolic in the water together at three in the morning. We had duck hunted together, squirrel hunted together, and deer hunted together. You get to know a person pretty well when you hunt with them, and we'd become close friends.

I cried for a few minutes and then wiped the tears from my eyes. I had to finish the journal, and the weather looked like it was about to change. I thought about another interesting time in my life and I began to write once again.

Typical of my resolve to make the tough deal came when the president of Good Financial Corporation would not let me have an appointment for six months. Talk about motivating me. When the appointed day finally arrived, I was postponed for six hours from my scheduled meeting time. Most people would have left. I simply danced. I was far too determined. When I finally saw Ken Good, he was perplexed that I had waited him out.

"You've got five minutes," he said harshly. He would not even shake my hand. There was no apology in his voice. There was only animosity.

"I know you are busy so I'll be brief," I said. "Mr. Good, you are known as the smartest real estate man in the area and I just have one question. What makes a good real estate man? What qualities do you look for in the person who brokers your deals?"

Ken looked at me for what seemed like my five minutes. Then he began to talk. He gave me a complete list of what it took to be a good broker but he went much further. He talked about the properties he'd bought and how he made his decisions. I listened as he listed off a number of things. He talked for a good ten minutes.

After he finished I said simply, "Now I know why we will do business. I offer..." and I went on to list the same traits he had just been talking about. Quickly, I said, "And here is the reason you will purchase this property from me."

I showed him the property I had come to present him and he taught me an unusual way to buy it. I delivered it to him that way.

Ken offered me a position as senior vice president for Good Financial Corporation. My five minutes turned into a lifelong friendship.

It was never about the money for me even though I accumulated large amounts, it was always about the deal. I would work harder on a little lease that would only pay $5.00 per month if it seemed impossible to put together. I loved the difficult deals, the ones that most people felt were impossible to make. Once I had made the difficult deal I always rewarded my family and myself. Part of the money made on every deal went toward family vacations to the mountains and to islands. We had some great vacations.

I tilted my hat back on my head as I thought of the great trips we had taken as a family. Now the kids were grown.

"Where had all the time gone?" I thought.

I looked around for a minute and picked up a rock, chunking it into the distance. Then I continued to write.

One of my worst moments was the day I took my firstborn, Jamie, to college. She had elected to go to Texas A&M after graduating high school. It was my alma mater and I was excited about her doing that, but I wasn't ready for the pain I experienced from her leaving home. I knew once she left home she would never come back except to visit. That is the way it is supposed to be. Jamie would make her own way in life and, as parents, Jackie's and my job was partially done. Jamie would now take what she had learned from us and make her own way in life. I never lived at home again after college and I knew Jamie wouldn't either. Nothing about my family life would ever be the same.

The trip to College Station had really taken its toll on me. Jackie had elected not to go as she didn't think she could bear to let Jamie go. We were both excited for Jamie and sad for ourselves.

Jamie had been with friends the night before leaving home and she slept during most of the four-hour trip. I looked at her. My little girl. My precious little girl. Leaving home for the first time, never to return. Tears welled up in my eyes and clouded my vision, and before I knew it I was recounting her beautiful little life to that point. This brought more tears. I began to sob. I just couldn't help it. The thought of my precious little girl, my firstborn, going off was too much. Who would protect her? She needed her daddy.

Fortunately by the time she woke I had composed myself after crying for three hours. I was able to send her on her way with a "You'll do great, girl." She'll never know the real pain I was feeling until her first-born leaves the nest.

It is not quite as difficult the second time around, when Jay left the nest. I was much more able to cope with that situation. It's easier with boys. Instinctively, fathers know that boys will be able to cope in the world. We know that our daughters will be able to cope too, but we have been their protectors for so long. Letting go was very difficult for me with both of my children.

I took the time to look up from my writing. The last sentence I had written had come crashing down into my senses. "Letting go was very difficult for me..." It was like a light bulb had gone off in my brain. Simple thought but really meaningful. "Letting go... was very difficult... for me..." For a few minutes I concentrated on this sentence. I had a hard time letting go of anything. I was like a snapping turtle that wouldn't let go until it thundered. In real estate, deals I should have let go of I worked on forever. Perseverance was listed as one of my strengths, but it was a weakness as well. There was a time to let go — especially of those things I wanted and loved. I wanted to keep them forever. It was about my trying to control my little piece of the world.

Plain and simple, there comes a time when you have to let go. I had been there before with my mother and Jamie, and I had to let go now. A person simply cannot control everything.

I walked from one side of the meadow to the other, going no place in particular. I was just clearing my mind. Finally I came back to my journal and began to write again.

My son, Jay, had grown into much more than the man I had hoped he would become. From his early childhood he seemed to know where he wanted to go and how he wanted to get there. My plans for the two of us to hunt and fish together never materialized. Maybe it was because of one particular time we went fishing and I accidentally caught his lip with a fishhook. Bless his little heart. We had to have a surgeon remove the hook. I felt so bad that I had done that to my son.

Many times in his young life I felt like he was smarter than me. He had a grasp for things that I had a difficult time understanding. He was very independent and made his own decisions. While I had hoped for a boy who loved nature like me, I got much, much more. I had a son who thought for himself, carried himself with dignity and poise, and who cared about others. Jay became my teacher, teaching me much more about life than I ever taught him. I have the utmost respect for my son.

I looked up from the journal and thought for a second about my son. It was true. Jay was a truly outstanding young man who was loved and respected by everyone who knew him because of what he was inside.

I had a long way to go in my journal so I began to write once again.

When I finally opened my own company I continued to do well. A friend of mine and I began to purchase apartments and became general partners in about 3,000 units. In 1986 the tax law changed and our apartments' value decreased by 25%, wiping out our equity. Friends in the business were taking bankruptcy right and left. My copartner was one of those. I fought it off and lost the large amount of cash I had in the bank. The pressure was tremendous. Some of my acquaintances were going to prison. Others were being investigated. Except for those who went through it, no one can ever communicate the absolute devastation that accompanied that 1986 tax law. I could never understand why the government did not choose to put a grandfather clause in the change. Had they done that, the Texas real estate market would not have fallen into the hole it remained in for the next ten years. The tax changes eventually contributed to the collapse of many savings and loan institutions as their asset values declined. Every real estate person was under suspicion. Every person related to that business suffered. Families were torn apart and long-term marriages ended. The pressure was just too great. It must have been somewhat like it was in the Great Depression. Fortunes were lost. People lost all they had. Some even took their own lives.

It was an unpredictable time. It was one time in my life I felt I had absolutely no control, and I did not. Still, I had made the choice to get into real estate. I had made the choice to buy apartments. I had made choices based on what I thought would happen and I learned another very important lesson: We cannot predict the future and we cannot control everything. Sometimes we have to learn to roll with the punches.

By now I was somewhat pissed off. Why I didn't know. It was never about the money for me. It was about the deal. Still, I was mad. Mad at the government. It was like when the poachers shot my cows.

There was nothing I could do about it. Why couldn't I let it go? To ease the pain I began to write about something else.

I killed my first squirrel with a BB gun and my first deer at age eleven with a British .308 I bought myself. My father did not hunt with me, nor did he teach me how to hunt. I learned with my BB gun. I shot my first deer while hunting with a friend of mine and his daddy. Mine was the only buck harvested on the particular hunt and there were fifteen seasoned hunters on that trip. Hunting became my passion. I was good at it. I loved the outdoors and the challenge of the hunt. Matching my wits against those of the wild animal was something I loved to do. But it was not challenging to me. By the time I was twenty I had given up the rifle in favor of the bow to hone my skills even more. I killed a six-point buck with a borrowed bow the first time I went into the woods. People said I was lucky, but I knew better. It wasn't until I met Dirk Ross, though, that I felt I had met a real teacher of the art of being in the outdoors and hunting. We had quickly become best friends.

"I'll write about Dirk later," I said out loud. "I'm not through with this other train of thought yet."

I have always been a high-energy individual. After college I continued to swim, compete, and teach lifesaving. I entered a Masters swimming program and went to nationals, where I placed in the top ten in ten different events. My coach tried to get me to specialize, but I'd rather have a good workout than win an event. I knew I could win if I focused on one event, but I did not have to prove that to anyone; least of all myself. In Texas I continually won most events I entered. I began to cross train and did a number of triathlons, winning my age group in some of them. I remember my son seeing me in pain in the run after having a nasty crash on a bicycle during a transition between the cycling phase and the run phase.

I was skinned up and limping and he said, "Why don't you quit?"

"I don't know how," was my answer.

Near the end of that race another competitor and I sprinted to the finish. I won that sprint.

I was always active with my children. Both of them. I taught them to swim. I helped them in school. I coached their soccer teams. I supported all their activities. I became president of the Booster Club and served in that capacity until both had graduated. My kids were great. Both were great athletes and both had a real enthusiasm for life and for learning. Jamie was a cheerleader for four years in high school. She was a joy to watch.

Jay was the most naturally talented athlete I had ever seen. He could do anything easily, just by watching someone else. He played football until a back injury sidelined him for good. He was elected president of his senior class and Mr. MacArthur High School. I was proud of him as he spoke at his high school graduation. Everyone was. He spoke from the heart like the leader he was.

I loved my children and I was proud of their accomplishments. More important, I was proud of the adults they were becoming. They were special.

Tears once again welled in my eyes and began to roll down my face.

"How did I get in this mess?" I asked aloud, then looked around. The clouds were continuing to build.

"Storm," I whispered aloud to no one in particular.

My body was shaking from the cold air and I felt the first wave of the sleet pepper me as I moved up the hill toward my spruce. I pulled my hat down tight as the wind pounded me. Sticking close under the canopies of the pine and spruce, I tried to keep as dry as possible. I looked to the east and could barely distinguish the meadow as the clouds had almost totally enveloped it in a foggy haze. I moved as quickly as possible, running from the protection of one tree to another, with each dash being greeted by sleet and snow. My body was soaked by the time I reached my spruce, and I was shaking so hard my teeth were chattering.

"Hypothermia," I muttered as I grabbed my shirt and began to wipe the water from my skin.

As soon as I felt dry enough I hopped in my mummy bag and pulled it around my head. The canvas bag on the outside of the down-filled bag acted as a barrier against any sleet and snow that made its way through the thick boughs of the spruce. I shivered for a good hour before I warmed in the comfort of the bag. I could hear the wind howling outside and occasionally heard thunder that seemed to be right on top of me. I tried to sleep and finally dozed. I woke and began to cry once again.

Since my father's death, my life had been in shambles. In seven years I had lost a huge amount of money and all my "net worth." I was fighting to stay alive financially. My mother had died after a lengthy illness.

Divorce was something I had never wanted. Just the thought of it made me sick. My parents had managed to stay together until death. Still, I had signed the paper a few days ago in Dallas. It was final. I was divorced. Twenty-eight years of marriage... over. Here I was in the mountains, penniless and alone. The thought caused me to become nauseated.

"Who are you, Jake?" I asked myself. "What will happen to you now? What will happen to your family? Why aren't you dancing? There is no music, but so what? You have danced before when there was no music. Your parents are dead. You've lost all your money. You have no wife. How will your kids react? What is the matter with you? Just who the hell are you? I don't know you anymore."

I tried not to cry but the tears would not stop. "Don't do that, Jake. Don't cry in the sleeping bag. It's down filled for heaven's sake and you know a wet bag loses its warmth. What is the matter with you?" The tears kept coming as I tried to will myself to sleep in a sleeping bag full of tears.

I slept fitfully, tossing and turning. Finally I fell into a deep sleep. Sometime in the night a loud noise like a lightning strike startled me. I opened my eyes into total darkness. There was no light anywhere. I tried to move but found myself trapped. I struggled for any rational thought.

"Where am I?" I thought.

Once again I tried to move, to turn. I could not. I felt a sudden unreasoning and overwhelming fear overtaking my body.

"There has to be a rational explanation for this," I thought. "Where am I?"

I could barely move, just shrug my shoulders a little. I was on my back and I was pinned down.

"By what?" My mind screamed for answers. "What has me pinned down?" I fought for answers. "If I could just turn over."

I fought. My breath was coming in short bursts. I could barely move my hands and I felt my surroundings.

"Oh my God, I'm in a coffin. I am buried alive. What is happening to me? Who put me here?"

I was sealed in and I couldn't move. I tried to struggle. It was useless.

"If I can just get my hands free. If I can just open the coffin. I need air."

The more I struggled, the more intense the feeling of not being able to breathe became. I felt claustrophobic. The feeling of being locked in a coffin overtook me. The air was thick and I was suffocating. I gasped for a breath. I tried to scream. I could not. Finally, with intense effort, I rolled over and became entangled in the material in the coffin. I clawed. I gasped for air. My body was drenched in sweat. Tears rolled down my face and I was petrified. I was dying and there was nothing I could do about it.

I fought, and the more I fought, the more trapped I became. There was no air to breathe. I was suffocating.

Finally I realized I had no control. All control was gone. There was no more fight in me. My energy was gone. The battle was over. I gave up and accepted my fate. I let go. I relaxed.

Finally I had peace.

Chapter 6

"Love makes everything that is heavy light."
Thomas P. Kempis

THE SKY WAS CLEAR, the sun almost overhead, and music filled the forest. The storm had passed hours earlier, leaving traces of its intensity. Tree branches were strewn around everywhere. A Steller's jay, from his perch atop a big boulder, glanced curiously at the rumpled pile of canvas under the big spruce tree. He flew down and landed on it for a closer look. His song blended in with the other sounds.

"Sounds. What are those sounds?" I listened intently. I recognized the sounds. "Somewhere in the distance birds are singing. Lots of birds. I hear a squirrel chattering. Wait a minute, they are not in the distance. They are close. Where am I?"

I moved my hands. I seemed to be tangled in something. My legs, my entire body was entangled. I moved my hips from side to side.

"Where am I? What? What am I tangled in?"

It came to me suddenly.

"I'm in my sleeping bag," I thought. "I am tangled in my sleeping bag. I'm alive."

I fought for the opening. It was like a wrestling match. Finally, I flipped over and was able to move my hands toward my face. I found the zipper on the side and managed to unzip it just a little bit. I was able to move my head up through the down bag and into the canvas that was covering my face. The stale air was freshening. I wrestled to push part of the canvas bivy sack away from my face. Fresh air streamed into my nostrils and I sucked it into my lungs. I was on my side and continued to unwrap myself from the mummy bag. I turned over on my back and looked up. In the tree above me were birds. All kinds of birds. I watched them as I continued to unwind the material from my body. I relaxed and laughed to myself. It had all been a nightmare. Or had it?

As I reflected on the previous night, it became evident to me that the dream was symbolic of something much bigger. I had fought for my very life. I had fought something I could not control. Finally, after a desperate fight for survival, I had given up. I had let go. I thought I had died.

The morning had brought a new life. The old Jake was no longer alive. The old Jake that scrapped and clawed to win had been beaten. The old Jake had let go. The old Jake had lost and in losing won a victory. A new Jake was born. It was a time to be happy and a time to rejoice. It was a time for discovery. It was a time to dance.

I watched the birds above me.

"What are you so happy about?" I said aloud.

A squirrel ran across a limb right over my head and leaped into another tree, then turned to look at me. He scolded me and I laughed.

The sun was out already. As I looked around I could see reminders of last night's storm. Snow and sleet were in patches all around the meadow and in shaded areas. I looked at the sun overhead and estimated the time to be about nine. I looked at my Timex. It was 1:00 P.M.

I put my hands behind my head and just lay there, looking at the sky through the spruce and listening to the serenade from the birds. The day was so different. Everything looked fresh and clean. The scents of the mountain meadow filled my nostrils.

"There has never been anything like the scent of a high mountain meadow after a storm," I said to the squirrel. "But you know that, don't you?"

A bird in a nearby tree caught my attention. I watched intently as it ate a grasshopper. As soon as it finished, it began to serenade me. I laughed out loud. It looked at me and sang louder, then, with a "watch me" attitude, it dove once again into the meadow and began to peck at the ground. Soon it flew back to the same perch with another, smaller grasshopper. It would hold the grasshopper with its claw and take bites with its beak. Then it would sing.

The entire planet was alive with things moving... things flying... things crawling. I watched as an ant crawled across my arm. I blew him off onto the soft ground under my spruce.

The birds continued to serenade me. I listened intently and as I watched they seemed to be telling me something. Then it dawned on me.

"God provides food for all the birds, but he doesn't put it into their nests. He expects them to get it for themselves." I reflected on that thought for a minute. "He provides the food. It's up to us to get it. He provides the water to sustain us. He provides building materials for our shelter, but he allows us to build for ourselves. He provides answers to our questions, but he expects us to seek the answers. And that is just what I am doing," I thought.

Answers were coming to me now. I also knew that questions I had not even thought of would be answered. It always happened that way when I was alone and searching. It always happened when I least expected it. And answers seemed to come to me best when I was in the forest. There was something about being close to the earth that seemed to encourage answers. It had been that way all through my life. I had a special wooded place as a little boy that I used to go to be by myself. As I grew up I always sought out such a place. I always found one, usually in a heavily wooded area.

Most people didn't understand the solitude I craved. When I went hunting I always liked to hunt by myself. I loved being alone in the woods. Only certain people understood my need. Shelton Eakin had understood. Dirk Ross also understood. It was no wonder that he had become my very best friend. He understood. From the first he understood.

I picked up my pad and began to write once again.

I remember the first time I met Dirk Ross. It was the summer of 1980. I was in Durango with my family, staying at our condominium at Tamarron. Hiking in the mountains by myself, I decided then and there that I wanted to meet a true mountain hunting guide and do a hunting pack trip into the wilderness. It had long been a dream of mine to go on such a trip. Of all the brochures for such a trip, one seemed to grab my attention more than others. I called the number and asked to meet with the outfitter. Dirk Ross showed up. I don't know what I was expecting, but I certainly wasn't expecting anyone like Dirk. He was friendly and outgoing, and I liked him immediately. More importantly, I trusted him completely. He would be the man I would hire to take me into the backwoods. I wanted to do a bow hunt and we planned a trip right then and there. I would find six bow hunters in Dallas to come with me. I could not wait for the next August to arrive.

The doctors and I drove to Durango together. There were five doctors and myself. We were looking forward to the adventure of a lifetime. We had no idea what was in store for us on that trip.

As Dirk was packing the mules that would carry our supplies into the wilderness, one mule named Sherry began to buck. Dirk threw his arms around the animal's neck and grabbed Sherry by the ear. Without warning, he bit it and Sherry quit bucking.

One of the doctors looked at me and said, "Did you see that?"

I nodded.

"Well, whatever you do," he said, "don't make him mad."

Dirk and I became the best of friends on that trip. It was an amazing experience being in the mountains with a true mountain man. He was simply born 100 years too late. He was an 1800s kind of man.

While we were walking around the edge of a meadow near some deadfall timber, a huge buck leaped up and started jumping over the deadfall. I was trying to get an arrow out of my quiver and nocked for a shot when I witnessed the most incredible sight I had ever seen. Dirk began chasing the buck across the deadfall, leaping from log to log. Then he lunged for the buck, grabbing its antlers and pulling its head to the side. With a swift motion, he released a razor-sharp nine-inch knife from his sheath and smoothly sliced the throat of the animal. He held on and blood squirted everywhere. Finally, the animal dropped to the ground, dead.

I could not believe what I had just witnessed. I was in total shock. I finally made my way over to where the animal lay and where Dirk was catching his breath.

All I could say was, "We don't kill 'em that way in Texas."

He looked back at me and said, "This ol' buck was sick. Couldn't you tell by the way he was moving?"

"I didn't notice anything different," I admitted. "I was trying to nock my arrow for a shot when you took off like a bullet, leaped like a madman from log to log, and landed on the animal's back. Then you took a knife out of your sheath and slit its throat. That's what I saw."

He laughed.

"Unbelievable. Just unbelievable," was all I could say.

I began to get ready for the long process of field dressing the deer. Dirk stopped me.

"We can't eat this deer," he said. "It is diseased. Too dangerous."

I thought he was joking.

Later I told the story to the doctors in camp. I'm not sure they believed me. I'm pretty sure I wouldn't have believed it. I saw it and I'm not sure I believed it. One of the doctors was a pathologist. "I want to see that animal," Dr. Ketchersid said.

I don't think any of them believed that the animal existed. After a long horseback ride back to where the animal lay with its throat slit from ear to ear, Ketch began the postmortem. After a quick examination of the entrails, he explained, "His liver shows signs of disease. He is full of infection. This meat is absolutely no good. Dirk was right."

What memories I still had of that trip. Dirk Ross became my hero, my mentor, and, more importantly, my close friend. We laughed as we tried to "cowboy up" aboard the molly mule Sherry on Rock Slide Meadow. She bucked us both off at 11,000 feet. We shared experiences. We laughed together. We cried together. We lay in the sun together. We walked for miles into aspen thickets and mountain meadows. We stalked animals into the dark timber. We traversed mountains on horseback following little-used game trails. We foot-raced up and down the mountains like two school buddies. He let me ride his buckskin. No other person had ever been allowed to ride his horse. In general, Dirk became my best friend and I his.

We spent summers together riding into the mountains. Half the time we camped without sleeping bags, often sleeping under the horse blankets. We carried little to no food, opting instead for a fishing line and hook we carried in a little plastic film container.

One time I remember telling Dirk that I was going to get my daughter a car for Christmas. He totally shocked me when he told me his Christmas gift to his family was going to be indoor plumbing.

I asked him what he would do if money were no object and he told me he would video the critters. That was the year I bought a video camera for him.

His little brother, Colt, often went with us and I learned to love the little guy as much as I did Dirk. He was tough and enthusiastic and was always learning from his big brother, whom he idolized. The three of us hunted an elk we named Old Sly because we could never seem to catch up with him. We never really wanted to. The hunt was what was important to the three of us. It was never about the kill.

In the fall I either hunted with Dirk or helped him with his hunters as an elk guide. Some of my greatest memories came from those experiences.

All of a sudden I was hungry. I dug my WhisperLite stove from my pack and lit it. Digging around I found some freeze-dried noodles I had packed and began the process of boiling water. Soon I was eating my first meal in five days. It tasted good. I scrounged further in the pack to see what I had brought for food. I had one more package of noodles and one package of beef stroganoff. The Boy Scout Motto, "Be Prepared," came to mind, and I laughed.

"I wasn't prepared for this trip," I thought. Still, the lesson of the birds was clear. "The food is here for the taking. I just have to go get it. I'll go catch some trout for dinner later in the day."

I stood and for the first time I could see the beauty around me. The sky was clear and the sun was shining. It felt good on my naked skin. I laughed for the first time in days. The blue spruce under which I had been sleeping seemed to be smiling at me. I hugged that tree.

"Thank you for providing shelter for me," I said aloud. Then without warning I added, "I love you. Thanks for providing the birds a place to perch, for providing a place for the squirrel to live. Thanks for providing a place for the bugs to crawl. Thanks for providing so much for all of us."

A gust of wind blew into the tree as I looked at its beautiful shape. The wind seemed to be bringing a message through the boughs of the spruce. It seemed to be talking to me. Its message seemed to be saying, "Follow............ Follow................"

I could never quite get the second word of the two-word message that seemed to be flowing from its limbs and boughs. The first word was clear: "Follow..."

"What does that mean?" I thought. "Follow. Follow what? Follow me? No, that's not it. What is that second word?"

All of a sudden I broke out in song.

"Away out here they have a name for earth and wind and fire. The earth is Tess, the fire Joe, and they call the wind Maria."

I was definitely feeling better, and, at least for now, the tears had stopped flowing. I grabbed my old hat, the hat with new meaning, and put it on. Daddy had taught me long ago that a person must respect and love himself before he was in a position to receive respect and love from other people. I sat down with my pen and journal and began to write about his teaching.

"It's like having a dollar in our pocket," Daddy said. "If someone wants a dollar from us and we have it, we can give it. If we don't have it, we can't give it. Respect and love are like that. If we have it for ourselves, we can give it. If we don't have it, we can't give it. Funny thing about both love and respect. We can really only receive it if we have it for ourselves. Oh, we can receive unsatisfying love and we can receive unsatisfying respect from others, but unless we love and respect ourselves, it will not fulfill our spirit. Life is to be lived learning who we are. Life is a journey into ourselves. It is a journey for a warrior, a warrior who will keep trying and continue to get into the

arena when all looks bleak. It is about finding out who we are and what we are about. Life is about defining us. It is not about reputation. Reputation is what people think we are. Character is about knowing ourselves... liking ourselves... loving ourselves. Life is about continuing to question who we are and what we are about. It is about continuing to try new things. It's continuing to learn. It's about stretching ourselves. It is a process. There is no set mark that we have to reach... no finish line. It continues all through our lives. Some people give up early. Some never learn to like themselves. Some continue to strive and never arrive. They feel they must continually win, and that is just not possible. We all have to lose to gain. Losing is the very act of gaining. For when we lose we are forced to try again. We are forced to dig into ourselves and determine what we could have done differently. We are forced to look into the very essence of our being. We never lose when we do that. We always win.

"Stretch yourself, Son. Always stretch yourself. Constantly strive to be a better person. Strive to learn about yourself. When things aren't going your way, seek the answers. Quiet your mind and ask yourself the hard questions. It is the journey to fulfillment. It is the journey to happiness. It is the journey to peace. It is a spiritual journey. Enjoy."

I felt an ant crawling across my arm and gently allowed it to crawl into the palm of my hand.

"I love you, little ant," I said as I watched it crawl off my hand and onto a boulder.

I had been given a new life. I had metaphorically died and now, with the old Jake gone, I was ready to receive answers. I still had a lot of work to do. It would be a long process... a rest-of-my-life process.

The pain I had felt from my divorce was still lingering inside me but the guilt was gone. It was time to begin a new life. It was time to, once again, shape my hat. It was time for the real Jake Billingsley to accept the responsibility for all his choices and move on. It was a time to learn to love myself again.

I felt love in my heart for everything I saw. I was dancing. The trees... the bushes... the sky... the water... the deer grazing in the meadow, became my dance partners as the music of love played in my heart.

For five more days I walked around in the wilderness naked. I touched every bush, coddled every blade of grass, and hugged every tree. I felt a part of it all. I felt the love of the universe as it came into my body. East Creek gave me fish from its stream. I loved them for giving their lives for me to have strength and I thanked them for it. I found wild strawberries along the bank and ate them, giving thanks for their being there for me.

The creek taught lessons every day. I learned about how stagnation came about by looking at a slew where the water was not running. The lesson was simple: Stay in the mainstream of life. Do not allow yourself to wallow in self-loathing, bad attitudes, and self-pity. That's when you stagnate.

A boulder in the middle of the creek taught me that one's strength of character can withstand any outside pressure. That boulder had withstood floods, debris banging up against it, and sand washing at its base. It stood tall, firmly planted, withstanding all onslaughts of nature.

The trees taught me lessons. Where there was shading of one tree over another, the tree being shaded fought for sunlight. The strongest trees grew side by side, neither shading the other. Relationships are like the trees. Each person in a relationship has to have room to grow... room to make choices... room to be themselves. If one person tries to dominate or abuse the other it has the effect of stunting the other's ability to grow as a person. The strongest relationships allow for the growth of each individual in that relationship. There is no shading of the other person... no dominance... no abuse... no desire to control. Rather there is a desire to see the other succeed and to be the best person they can be. They stand side by side and grow strong individually.

Had I stunted Jackie's growth? Had she stunted mine? Was this what had happened to our marriage? Is this what they mean when they say "we grew in different directions"?

It was a time to learn new lessons... to reflect on the past and to look forward to the future. Love was all around me.

From the squirrels, I learned the sheer joy of living. From the fawn, the joy of discovery. From the birds, the joy of singing. From the meadow, the smells of plants, flowers, and even weeds. Nature has a way of teaching lessons. We just don't take the time to see the beauty in all things. The hawk swoops down on the field mouse and the field mouse gives its life to the hawk. God put the field mouse in the meadow. God put the hawk in the sky. It is the way of nature. One life dies so another can live. It dawned on me that an old life can die and a new one could begin. We had to be willing to give up the old life.

A tree is hit by lightning, ignites, and gives forth its seeds to the ground. As it dies, a family of squirrels moves into the hollow. As it finally crumbles, it provides mulch and food for the other plants. Worms find the dead tree. Termites too. The worms and termites I use to catch the fish. One dies, another lives. In death there is life. It is the cycle. The cycle of life.

On the fifth day after my "resurrection" I had a chance meeting with an old friend of mine. I was walking through the woods, naked as usual, when I spotted a huge bull elk on the other side of a slight ridge, no more than twenty yards away. I recognized the bull elk immediately. It was Old Sly.

He didn't see me at first. The wind was in my favor and for that I was thankful. I froze in my tracks and immediately began to appreciate his beauty. Only last year Dirk and I had seen him in heavy timber on a south-facing slope.

I whispered, "There you are, old boy. Just as beautiful as ever. I guess you are getting ready to look for cows. It's about that time of year. You are so very strong and beautiful. I would like to look at you for a few minutes if that's alright."

He stopped and looked in my direction. I remained as if frozen to the spot. His eyes focused on me, and I could feel his energy and strength.

"You are the most beautiful animal in the forest," I continued in a soft whisper. "I love you. I can feel your energy and strength."

He continued to look at me. His eyes penetrated into mine, and I felt a warmth engulf my body. The feeling was like when I was a little boy and my mother would hold me close and rock me. My eyes looked deeper into his and suddenly I noticed a mystical, mist-like glow around his entire body. It followed the curvature of his gloriously strong body and antlers. It rose like steam, darker close to his body, then lighter farther away. As I watched, the misty glow turned from a gray shade to an almost purple color. It reached out farther and farther from his body. At first only a few inches, then ten, then eighteen. As I stood in wonder I could sense a feeling of total oneness with him. It was more than that. The misty glow was almost cloud-like as it moved in my direction and seemed to penetrate all parts of the forest. It rose from the trees, the plants, the bushes, even the rocks, and I became a part of it. It was a complete feeling... a feeling of being part of something bigger than I could ever imagine. It was a feeling of oneness with all things. I felt tears come into my eyes and flow down my cheeks.

Beautiful, golden aspen leaves began to fall all around me and a gust of wind on my back told me my scent was being carried into his nostrils. Still, he did not move. He just stood there looking at me and I at him.

I whispered once again, "Thank you, thank you for this moment. Thank you for his feeling. Would you just let me do one more thing? Would you just allow me to feed you something? To get close to you?"

With that I slowly knelt down and picked a clump of grass near my right foot. I never took my eyes off him as I slowly straightened up. One tiny step at a time I slowly moved in his direction. I was in a dreamlike state. My eyes were taking in all that was around me but my body was a part of it all. It was like I was watching a movie, while at the same time being a part of it.

I continued to talk to Old Sly. "I have hunted you for a lot of years. I have been close to you before. You and I have a connection. We are here at this time for a reason. We are sharing something special together. Please let me feed you."

Step by baby step, I closed the gap between Old Sly and myself. Fifteen yards. Ten yards. Five yards. Still he did not move. Three yards. Two. I was so close. His body heat and scent was wrapping me in a cocoon of warmth. I offered him the grass by extending my arm in his direction. He looked at it. He looked at me. There was no fear in his body. There was no nervousness. He stood there. Watching me.

I took one more step in his direction and he turned his head and took a step away from me. Then another. He stopped. Looked back at me. I took a step toward him again. Once again he turned his head and this time began to move away slowly. As he moved uphill, I continued to talk to him.

"Thank you for taking the time to let me get close to you. Thank you for letting me feel your love and warmth. Thank you. Thank you. Thank you."

Tears were rolling down my cheeks... big tears. They were landing on my shoulders, my arms, and even my feet. And I was grinning. I couldn't have stopped if I had tried and I didn't want to try.

At about ten yards, Old Sly stopped and looked back at me. I'll never forget that moment. It is etched in my memory forever. He had felt it all too. He had been a part of my spiritual journey into the oneness of all things. It was as much a mystery to him as it was to me. He moved over the ridge and out of sight. The mist moved off with him and I was left alone in the forest once again. This time I knew that I was not alone. I was with the trees. I was with the plants. I was with the rocks. I was a part of them and they were a part of me. It felt good. I felt good. In fact, I felt better than I had felt in my entire life.

For the next two days there wasn't a tree in the forest I didn't hug. I loved everything I saw. It was a totally incredible experience.

On the afternoon of the second day after my meeting with Old Sly, I heard a familiar voice say, "You ready to come home yet?"

When I looked around, Dirk was sitting on top of his buckskin, just grinning at me.

"Never entered my mind," I answered.

"Well, I came to git you. That body of yours has been scaring all the game clean out of these parts. I'm not sure they'll ever come back."

I laughed. "Good to see you, too, Dirk. I see you brought an extra horse. Is that for me?"

"It is if you want it."

"How did you find me?"

"I just back followed the tracks of all the animals that was leaving the area. Besides, I figured you to be up here somewhere. You look a might bit skinnier than you did the last time I saw you."

"How long have I been gone?" I asked.

"Pretty close to two weeks, I guess. I figured you might be ready to come out of the mountains by now."

"I think I am," I said, not totally sure myself. "Why don't you climb down out of that saddle and set a spell while I gather some stuff up. Sorry I can't offer you anything to eat. I've been living on brookies and strawberries and I only fish when I'm hungry."

"I brought my own, thank you. But I'm not crawling off this horse till you put your pants on."

I rummaged around and finally found my pants, shirt, and underwear at the bottom of my sleeping bag. I dressed quickly, noticing that my pants were all but falling off.

"Boy, I have really lost the weight," I said.

Dirk climbed down off the buckskin and produced some beef jerky for me to chew on.

"When you're ready, we'll talk. If you never git ready, well, that's all right too."

That was Dirk, my best friend. He was there for me if I needed him. Yet he didn't interfere. He had taken time to look for me in the mountains and I knew that he was probably worried about me, but he never let on. I never really knew how he found me. I was a good four or more hours from civilization. I had been gone for nearly two weeks and the rain had long washed out any tracks I may have made. Still, Dirk found me. He had this uncanny way of knowing where to go and when. He was a true mountain man. I trusted him completely. I relied on his judgment. He was my teacher.

"Just one thing I want to say before I leave this place, Dirk. This is a special place for me. I love everything in it. That includes you, Dirk. Do you understand that?" I felt my eyes tear up as I looked at the rugged man in the beat-up cowboy hat as he stood in front of me and handed me the reins of my horse.

"I understand," he said gently. "I love you, too. Now tie that bedroll on the back of that horse and let's hightail it down the mountain. We can just about make it down by dark."

I walked over to him and gave him a big hug. He hugged me back, then pushed me away and socked me in the stomach.

"Damn, Jake, what if somebody rode up about now? You and I hugging and all."

He climbed in the saddle and the buckskin sauntered off down the trail. I tied the bedroll on the back of the bay and followed him. I stopped where the trail met the timber and took one last long look around. Something magical had happened in this place. Something I would never forget.

Chapter 7

"It is with true love as it is with ghosts;
everyone talks about it, but few have seen it."
Francois De La Rochefoucauld

I DROVE BACK to Dallas with complete resolve. I knew what I had to face and I was more than ready to take the necessary steps. I knew that I could not be responsible for anyone's happiness but my own. The alone time had taught me that. It had also taught me that material things really have no value. None. Only those things that enhance the spirit are valuable. Very quickly I deeded my free and clear dream home to Jackie. I would continue to keep the debt.

As I continued my commercial real estate career, I was haunted by the word follow. Follow who? Follow what? What did it mean?

A friend told me that a woman for whom I had the utmost respect had recently gone through a divorce proceeding also. When he told me, I was excited. I had known Virginia Adams for a number of years. We had served on community boards together and I really liked her personality. Most importantly, though, I respected her ability to get things done. She never put off anything. She took on each task as a personal challenge and moved forward constantly. She was petite and vivacious and I was excited about the possibility of dating her.

It was difficult to find her phone number but finally I convinced one of her friends that we could help each other through this tough time in our lives. It was a rather lame excuse I had used, but hey, it worked. I was able to get her on the phone.

"Virginia, it's Jake Billingsley. How are you?" I said when I finally heard her voice.

"Just running off to class, Jake. Can you call me back later?"

"Sure, what time is good for you?"

"Could you make it about 9:30? I should be back by then."

She sounded great. She was in the healing phase of her divorce also and I found out when we finally talked that she had enrolled in a community college and had plans to get her college degree. I admired her for that. Instead of waiting and hoping, this girl had taken the bull by the horns and was in the process of rebuilding her own life after her thirty-year marriage ended. She was starting over with nothing. Her personality had never seemed like it fit her name. Virginia just did not fit and I asked her if I could call her Jeni. She told me that she was a Jeni growing up... that her parents had called her that. It was settled... she was to be a Jeni once again. The name fit her. Change in name and change in life.

What began as a friendship soon blossomed into a magical relationship. What began as two friends helping each other through hard times emerged as something very special. Jeni was strong and determined. No man was ever going to push her around. She knew what she wanted and was bound and determined to get it for herself. She was a totally independent woman. The more I was around her the more I wanted to be around her.

When I was near her I felt like a high school boy. Sometimes I even felt like I was in grade school. I was totally attracted to her. She could be a little girl, a mother, the prom queen, and a gifted counselor. We talked for hours on the phone and I never tired of her conversation.

We were compatible on all levels. Emotionally we were perfect for one another. We had issues to work through and it helped to have a compassionate person to talk to. Intellectually we were equals. We discussed nearly every subject, arguing about many, but in a spirit of fun. She held her ground in every argument. Spiritually we were both

Christians, but more than that, we could talk about all parts of spirituality. Sometimes we even argued about religion but they were healthy, learning type arguments. Physically we were perfect for one another. She matched my passion and made me feel wanted for who I was, not what I could do for her.

Dr. Wayne Dyer put it this way: "Love is the ability and willingness to allow those that you care for to be what they choose for themselves, without any insistence that they satisfy you."

I let go. I gave myself to her totally... completely. I let her see all my weaknesses as well as my strengths. I became, for the first time in my life, vulnerable. It was a wonderful feeling. I was determined to follow love no matter what the cost.

Our lovemaking was surreal... almost spiritual. The chemistry was definitely there. But something else was there too. When we were together the world stopped. Being with her was like uncovering layers in my soul previously unexplored. And with the peeling back of each layer a new meaning billowed, blending with what was already there and making it better. Being with her allowed me to see things I had never seen before through eyes I had never looked through before. She was the inspiration for poems.

Morning Music

The morning breaks
   quiet, soft, mistily
The warmth of your touch
   The sound of your breathing
Deep — peaceful
   The music of the morning fills my being with mystery
Not knowing what the day will bring
   Not caring
So long as you are with me.

The sun breaks through and sends its beautiful streamers through the mist
   Still you sleep
I cannot help but gently caress your skin
   So beautiful, so soft
Birds, sensing the beauty of the moment, begin their morning serenade
   You are there — beautifully peaceful
All is well

Touching, caressing, holding, being oh so careful
   Gently kissing your cheek and you stir
Eyes open slowly — sleepy — happy eyes
   A slight smile and a slow gentle stretch
My love is awakening
   The music of the birds fills the room
The day will be wonderful — they know it too
   You are with me.

No words
   Words aren't needed
A gentle touch
   A sleepy smile
The eyes that are so full of love looking into mine
   My heart opens and you come in as you've done so many times before
My day is beginning — my life is freshening — my love is overwhelming
   And you, my darling Jeni, create my music for the day.

   Jakespeare

By this time I had begun to follow my intuition totally. The mountain experience had told me to "follow" and I was on a path of self-discovery. My journey was taking me into venues I had never been before. It was sending me into bookstores where books would literally fall off the shelf onto the floor in front of me. I studied all the major philosophies and religions of the world. I could share these with Jeni and we discussed them at length. I began to call my quest my "follow" quest. I had been given the message to follow and I thought I was doing a pretty good job of it.

I read everything I could get my hands on. I continued my studies of religions and philosophies and read every book I could find on the subject. It bothered some of my Christian friends that I would read anything but Christian books. I wondered why that was all they were reading. There was so much to learn from others. I studied everything. As I took in information and processed it, I kept that which I felt applied to me and discarded the rest.

An example was crystals. I studied the crystals. I read about them. I read testimonials of people who believed in them. I discarded the theory of crystals only after study as something that I did not need. I was equally certain for many other people the crystals were a good thing. Just not for me. I was totally open to new ideas and philosophies. I planned to follow where I was being led and I was enjoying the journey.

Friends told me that I should be enjoying more young, hot women. They wondered why I didn't care to date any of them. I tried, but shallow conversations were not my bag. In fact I was bored by them. I was at a different place in my life. Getting laid just to get laid had no appeal to me. Making love with Jeni did. She was older, only two years my junior, and certainly wiser, smarter, and prettier than any girl I had ever met.

My life had changed so drastically that I hardly recognized myself. I was following something. I wasn't sure what. I just knew I would follow wherever my intuition told me to go.

I had been, prior to my father's death, a man who never cried. Forty-one years and never a tear. It had all changed in March of 1982. I allowed myself to feel every emotion and I found myself crying at movies. I went from a man of great wealth to a pauper... from a man who had a wonderful wife and family to a bachelor... from a man who knew what he wanted and how to get it to a man who was shaping his hat. I was determined to shape it right. I was determined to shape it with respect and love. I was determined to discover me, to love me, and to find my purpose in life. I was questioning everything in my life... my values... my beliefs. I had read of the "middle-age crazies." Maybe that was what I was going through. All I knew for sure was that I felt as if I was living life to the fullest. God had a plan for me and as long as I kept following my intuition, I would find it.

I knew that my connection to Jeni was real. I loved the way she looked. She was petite, about 5'2" and weighing 104 pounds. She had a teeny tiny waist and the most beautiful legs I had ever seen. Her blonde hair fell shoulder length and always seemed just a little rumpled. I loved that look. She looked like a teenager... the girl next door... a best friend. I loved the way she walked and carried herself. She walked with confidence... the confidence of a woman who knew who she was and what she was about. Her shoulders were back and her posture was perfect. I loved to watch her walk. I just loved to watch her.

I loved to watch her interact with people. She had all the people skills in the world and people loved to be around her. Her personality shined like a light in a fog and illuminated everyone that came near her. She was a Leo by the sign of the zodiac. She was born August 17th... my sister's birthday. I was born on August 21st. Two Leos. Two people who liked the same things. Two positive people. It was magical.

Of all the things I loved about her I think her eyes were the most enchanting. When I looked into them I was totally mesmerized. Sometimes they were childlike and playful. Sometimes they were soulful and sincere. Sometimes they were vampish and sexy. I never knew which Jeni I was going to be with until I looked into her eyes... those beautiful green eyes. One of my favorite things to do was to get really close to her. Nose to nose we would whisper and talk for hours on end. It was that intimacy that I craved and she gave it to me in bucket loads.

We continued to date. We dated for months. The months turned to a couple of years. She was determined to stay independent and heal completely from her divorce. Equally important she was determined that we should date other people. I tried but it was never right. It never felt good to me. Younger women seemed to be too self absorbed and older ones seemed to be carrying too much baggage. After being with Jeni every one of them seemed boring. I was totally unfulfilled being around anyone but her. I was in love. Real love. Deep spiritual love. It was mystical and it was magical.

Jeni tried dating others too but had the same problem. It seemed that fate had brought us together. We would have to play the cards we were dealt as long as it lasted.

The more I was around her the more convinced I was that she held the key that fit my lock. She was my soul mate... my gift from God... the person I was supposed to be with the rest of my life... the person with whom I would grow and from whom I would learn. She would be my teacher and I hers. With her near me I could face anything... everything. We would be like two trees in the forest growing side by side, neither shading the other. We would not stunt the other's growth. We would learn together. Our roots would grow deep in love.

We bounced things off each other because there was so much respect for the other's opinion. There was no jealousy. There was no baggage. There was only nurturing and touching and love. Deep love. Jeni allowed me to be me and she loved me in spite of my shortcomings. She did not want to change me. She encouraged me to feel, to touch, and to show emotion. We shared those feelings. She allowed me to be free and I felt that freedom. It was like looking in a mirror. The more I loved Jeni, the more she loved me back. She was as spontaneous as I was. We lived in the moment. There is no need to dream of the future or live in the past. Our moment is now and we both lived it and continue to live it as it happens.

Chapter 8

"Life is a mystery, not a problem to be solved."
Albert Einstein

JAMIE HAD GRADUATED from Texas A&M and, for her graduation present, wanted to go into the mountains with me on a horseback trip. It thrilled me that she wanted to do that. I had taken Jay on a similar trip a few years earlier with Dirk and Colt, and she was bound and determined that he was not the only one to get that trip. Since the divorce, Jamie and I had spent little time together, and I knew a trip like this would bring us close once again. She seemed to love the mountains almost as much as I did and had contemplated moving to Colorado after she graduated.

Our week-long horseback journey was to begin with a couple of days along the Pine River, then up over the Continental Divide, and back down the Vallecito River. I knew she would see some of the most beautiful country in the world. We would fish in the cold mountain lakes and camp anywhere we found a suitable spot.

Jamie had dated a number of cowboys in high school and college and basically had a "thing" for cowboys. I told her on the trip that she would have an opportunity to meet a real cowboy when we came down from the mountain. I told her that not only was he a real cowboy, this man was all man. I was describing Colt Ross and I meant every word I said. I had watched that boy grow up. He was tough, fair, and all man. Not only that, he was a handsome man. He was a half-inch shy of six foot four, broad in the shoulder and narrow at the hip. Colt had a smile that would melt the snow and he used it seemingly all the time. Girls fell all over the athletic Colt Ross.

After a week in the mountains, Jamie was totally ready to get to a spot where she could take a shower and sleep in a good bed. She didn't care whether she ever rode a horse again. We rode in after dark and there, at the corral, was none other than Colt Ross cooking hamburgers for a group, mostly girls. The firelight accented his handsome features. I introduced Jamie to him. Right then and there I saw more sparks in their looks than there were in the campfire. It wasn't long before Jamie sidled up to me and whispered, "I think I like it here."

Later she asked me if she could go scouting for elk with Colt the next morning. He would pick her up before dawn and they would saddle up and go back into the mountains. I said, "Jamie, I thought you were tired of the mountains. I thought you said you might never ride a horse again. What gives?"

She just grinned.

Jamie moved to Durango right after she graduated from Texas A&M. It seemed like such a good idea to me that I bought a used travel trailer and moved there too. I could just drag my home with me. I justified it by saying that Dirk had wanted me to write a book for him as a ghostwriter anyway. I loved living in Colorado and took a job at Purgatory Ski Mountain selling condominiums. Jeni stayed in Dallas to finish her education.

I went back to Dallas periodically and during the Christmas season of '91 Jeni and I planned to cross-country ski in the San Juans. As we left Dallas, Jeni began to feel puny. On the drive from Dallas to Durango she became feverish and by the time we arrived at our cabin at about nine in the evening she had developed a full case of the flu. The temperature gauge read –10 degrees when we moved into our secluded little cabin in the mountains. We had planned a romantic trip. It just didn't work out that way.

Our cabin was warm and toasty and Jeni went right to bed while I unpacked everything from the car. I finally crawled in bed about midnight but was awakened a few hours later by a terrible odor that was easily recognizable. A family of skunks had taken up residency under our romantic little hideaway. There we were. All of us. Jake, sick Jeni, and a family of skunks all trying to share the same space. The little cabin wasn't big enough for all of us and the little black and white critters definitely had the advantage. It was hysterical... We left with all of our clothes as well as our bodies reeking. It was not the most romantic of all the places I have been. Imagine poor Jeni with the flu and having to put up with all that. If I hadn't known just how special Jeni was before that, I would have known it then. She never complained. She just laughed along with me. We found another cabin and she slept for three days.

Things happened pretty fast after that. Jamie and Colt were married in a wonderful ceremony on the banks of Lake Vallecito. It was a wedding fit for a cowboy and his cowgirl. The groom, groomsmen, and father of the bride rode in on horseback. The bride came in a stagecoach. The only glitch in the entire wedding was after I helped Jamie out of the stagecoach I forgot to give the wedding bouquet back to her. I ended up carrying it down the aisle. A cowboy in a black hat carrying a bouquet down the aisle. Go figure.

Dirk proposed that I go to Siberia with him on an adventure trip where he would hunt grizzly bear and Maral stag with a bow. I would film the trip, which would include several other hunters.

Did I go? You bet. It was an adventure, wasn't it?

When we returned I wrote my first published article. I was so proud.

AN AMERICAN MOUNTAIN MAN IN RUSSIA
By Jake Billingsley

The American mountain man stood motionless in the Siberian tundra... ice clinging to his stocking-covered feet. Something moved just below the bench on which he stood and I focused the video camera as antlers appeared. I counted twelve points, six on each side. Clearly a trophy.

On the snow-covered slope to my left, and no more than thirty feet from me, a cow appeared, then another. The bull crested the bench not more than twenty feet from the hunter.

The mountain man stood statue still, his longbow slightly canted, an arrow resting on the top of his glove-covered hand. The distance between prey and hunter narrowed as the bull continued his determined walk, looking for the cow he was sure was there. Twelve feet from the mountain man he stopped abruptly and stared... confused. Neither predator nor prey moved. Finally, the bull elk turned away from the hunter, looked back once, and then ambled off. The mountain man drew the arrow, knowing he had the perfect shot.

The decision to go to Siberia in September 1992 with Dirk Ross, president of Mountain Man Enterprises, a Colorado-based holding company for his video production business and his outfitting business, had been an easy one.

Dirk is an 1850s mountain man living in 1992. He has spent all of his thirty-six years hunting, trapping, and fishing in the San Juan Mountains of southern Colorado where he has owned and operated Rocky Mountain Outfitters for the past fifteen years. He is arguably the best elk hunter in America today and has directed and produced what have been termed by the experts as the best outdoor hunting videos in the world, which he sells under the name Mountain Man Enterprises.

Dirk had said during our brief telephone conversation, "Imagine, Jake, we will have the opportunity to get to know the people of rural Russia. Not only will we hunt with the best hunters in Siberia, we'll take video cameras and record the entire trip. Russia is beginning to open its doors to tourism and encouraging American hunters to come to areas of Siberia that were previously hunted only by the Russian elite."

"Sounds good," I said, "When do we leave?"

I had hunted with Dirk Ross for more than ten years. It never occurred to me to question the sanity of the idea.

I'm not quite sure the Russian people at Red Square in Moscow were ready for the mountain man. Sporting a full beard and dressed in a worn-out cowboy hat complete with elk horn hat band, sheepskin vest, and rabbit fur gaiters, Dirk created quite a stir everywhere he went. It seemed to me that as many pictures were made of him as of the "goose stepping" changing of the guard at Lenin's tomb. Dirk is a handsomely rugged man who stands a couple of inches over six feet and weighs about ten pounds short of two hundred. Imagine Jeremiah Johnson in Russia, and you've got the picture.

When we arrived in Irkutsk, Siberia (pronounced Iricrucks), the eight of us on a tour booked through Russia Hunt of San Antonio, Texas, had passed through fourteen time zones. Through our tour guide and interpreter, Masha Rukhina, we were split into four groups of two, with each group going into a separate area. We would not see each other again for twelve days. I was envisioning the salt mines and never seeing my family again.

Two groups were immediately whisked away in a military helicopter. One group was put in a fast flying cargo plane, and Dirk and I settled into the back of a car for a four-hour automobile ride. Deema, a director of hunting and forestry activities in an area about the size of nine counties in the United States, was one of our guides for the week. He spoke very little English, which made for some very animated conversations.

The countryside in Siberia made me imagine what America must have looked like in the early 1900s. There were no fences at all; the only blight on the beautiful Siberian countryside was the crisscrossing of modern power lines. Hay was stacked by hand. Grazing cattle were tended by men and women on horseback.

We passed everything on the highway (about like one of our well-patched Texas farm to market roads) including many motorcycles with sidecars. Our driver, Carda, darted in and out of the highway traffic with the precision of a professional race car driver. I recited the Lord's Prayer more on that four-hour trip than in forty years of church on Sunday mornings.

Finally we stopped in a small rural village and unloaded our gear into a helicopter, which Dirk appropriately named "the Russian mule." For an hour and a half we flew down the Oka River to what was to be our base camp. Here we met our other guide, Anatole (Deema called him Tole, which rhymes with holy), supposedly one of the very best trappers and hunters in Siberia. We were the first

Americans Tole had ever met. He understood no English — none at all. The game of charades began.

After a dinner of potatoes, cabbage, and meat stew we feasted on *clep* (bread) and *bushnickle* (wild berries) with a milk and sugar topping. Using a book the guides had in camp, we found that the animals we call elk are called Maral stags in Siberia. What we call moose, the Siberians call elk. Confusing? Yes, but it didn't take us long to communicate to them that Dirk wanted to take a Maral stag with his longbow. Few hunters had ever hunted with a bow in Siberia. Deema and Tole were extremely skeptical.

During the next few days we fell in love with Siberia, a country full of natural resources. Where we were hunting on the Oka River there is moss sometimes waist deep that makes the best natural caulking and insulation in their near perfectly built lodge pole hunting domes (all homes are called domes). There are berries in abundance, and the guides were constantly picking them for our desserts. *Chay* (tea) was made from the leaves and stems of several plants native to the area. Our guides drank no cold water at all, preferring to drink hot chay. Also in great abundance were pinon trees loaded with pine nuts, which provide a living for many of the rural Siberian people. The bark of the birch tree, so plentiful in Siberia, is used for everything from shelter to fire starter.

Tole broke out his Maral stag bugle, which was made of birch bark in one long strip about six inches wide and four feet long. The birch is harvested in the month of May and allowed to dry in a roll. When ready to use, the birch is simply pulled out into a bugle and a birch reed installed. The tone is excellent for a big bull and Tole was a master in his bugling. Remembering the dueling banjo scene in *Deliverance*, I convinced Dirk to bugle like a big bull. Tole was impressed when Dirk, using nothing but his lungs and mouth, bugled and chuckled.

Dirk then demonstrated cow talk using a diaphragm in his mouth. The guides didn't understand, and after acting out a Maral stag with horns, Dirk, using a feminine walk and pursed lips, demonstrated the difference between a bull and a cow. Dustin Hoffman as "Tootsie" couldn't have done better. Watching the mountain man swivel his hips, flirt with his eyes, and purse his lips was one of the highlights of the trip, which I'm happy to say, was recorded on video. One couldn't help but wonder if this was the way the mountain men of the 1800s communicated with the American Indians. The guides indicated that cow elk in Russia do not talk.

"Could that be?" I asked Dirk.

"We are surely going to find out," Dirk said with a grin. "I can't imagine it though."

On the second afternoon of our hunt we moved up the river to an old geological cabin where we found the remains of core samples by the thousands. Our move was to be near the tundra where the snow was plentiful and where we hoped to find the Maral stag.

Early the next morning, after a breakfast of chay, clep, and a macaroni and meat meal, we began a hard thirty-minute walk toward the tundra. As we neared our objective, we slowed to hunting speed. Tole bugled. In the early morning dawn we could see tracks and sign, including fresh bear scat, which caused a shiver to run the length of my spine. I chuckled to myself as I thought of the advice given me by a friend who had hunted grizzlies in Alaska. "The bad news is," he had said with a grin, "you can't outrun a grizzly. They can outrun a horse for a short distance. The good news is you don't have to. You just have to be able to outrun the person you are with."

Moving into a pocket where two drainage areas met, Tole continued to bugle at regular intervals. The creeks and streams, plentiful in that area, were covered with ice and snow. It was cold. From the canyon to our left, we heard the bugle of a Maral stag. Again he bugled as we all agreed on his direction. The hunt was beginning. Dirk took the lead and immediately sat down to discard his boots in favor of his stocking feet. Not me, my boots were warm and felt good. My job was to work the video and record the events and I figured to do it with warm feet. The guides tried to stop Dirk with no success and I indicated to them that he was a little crazy. I mean here we were, ice and snow all over the ground, and the man with the longbow was discarding his boots because they were too noisy.

The plan was a simple one, Tole and Deema were to stay well back of us and bugle. I was to follow Dirk at about twenty-five feet and keep the camera in action.

We moved forward... carefully. After a five-hundred-yard stalk, we could see the bull and a few cows in a creek bottom just to our left. Carefully studying the wind, we crept forward. Dirk cow talked and the bull started in his direction. I readied the camera for action and positioned myself with my back to a birch tree. Tole bugled and interestingly enough one of the cows started toward him. The bull, in a jealous rage, positioned himself between her and Tole, moving her back to the herd and then moving the entire herd up the mountain. He was bellowing every minute or so and Tole answered just as often.

We followed, noticing the bull was having a major problem with one of the cows. She was fickle and had her sights set on Tole. The bull had to keep pushing her onward further and further up the mountain and away from Tole. The problem was that Tole and Deema were following along after Dirk and I, and literally driving the animals away.

Backing off, Dirk and I went back for another animated conversation with Tole and Deema. I videoed as Dirk explained what was happening to our hunt by poking sticks into the frozen ground. Bow hunters are known for their patience and it was certainly the mountain man's long suit on that day. I couldn't help but laugh as Dirk pointed to five sticks.

"Maral stag," he said, poking one stick in the ground.

"Cows," he said, pursing his lips and moving his hips as he inserted four more sticks into the ice and snow.

"Tole," he pointed to another stick signifying Tole.

"Tole wooeeii," he demonstrated Tole bugling. With pursed lips and wiggly hips, he pointed to the sticks that represented the cows.

"Cow like Tole. Try to go to Tole. Think Tole big and strong."

Tole and Deema understood. Tole almost blushed.

"Maral stag have trouble with cow in love with Tole. Move away."

Demonstrating where he wanted Tole and Deema to stay until we could get into pressure range, Dirk and I moved forward. We had to move fast now because the animals were about five hundred yards away. Tole stayed and bugled. The Maral stag bugled back, and we moved out at a brisk pace and closed to within one hundred yards before we began what was to be our final stalk.

At about sixty yards we were placing one foot slowly in front of the other and rolling to the outside, walking on cat feet. We stopped. Tole bugled and the bull answered.

Dirk looked back at me. "Watch this," he whispered. He cow talked.

The bull went into a frenzy and Dirk pulled an arrow from his sheepskin quiver as he grinned back at me.

We positioned ourselves. I was in back of him about twenty feet as he nocked the arrow. He let out a small bull bugle and the bull went into a rage. From my position I could hear him tearing up a tree as he bellowed back.

I looked behind me and saw our Siberian friends creeping in as was the plan. Tole would bugle no more, and they would take position about fifty feet from me and watch. Dirk was now in charge as I've seen him so many times before. He had the bull on a string. It was a pleasure to watch him work. He would cow talk, sending his cow talk in all directions. Then he would do a small bull bugle and we would watch the herd bull go into a tirade. He would bellow. He would chuckle. He would tear brush.

He was not coming any closer, but he was not moving away.

Dirk bugled again and one of the cows broke from the herd, talking all the time. The others began talking and the entire mountain filled with their chatter. As I watched, the herd bull, posturing all the time, continued to move between the cows and us. He moved the entire herd off over the bench we were on and we watched them disappear from view. We followed.

Dirk was in the middle of an opening using cow talk when I first saw the antlers. He froze into the mountain as if planted there. The agitated bull walked on determined feet. He was through talking. He was finished with herding. He would whip that young bull and take the cows he knew were his for the taking. No more running.

At twelve feet he saw Dirk. They stood almost nose-to-nose for a long minute, then the bull stepped to his left and offered the perfect lung shot. I expected the familiar twang.

Instead I heard, "Gotcha, big boy," accompanied by a wonderful laugh. Then he added, "Boy, that was some hunt, wasn't it, Jake?"

The bull crashed down the hill in the direction of Tole and Deema.

The acting was easily understood. Tole and Deema wanted to know why he didn't shoot.

Communicating a philosophy to someone who speaks your language is hard enough, but when trying it with someone who doesn't speak your language the task is next to impossible. It is easy to point at bread and say "bread" while the other says "clep." It doesn't take a brain surgeon to point at a picture of an elk and say "elk" while the other says "Maral stag." A hunting philosophy would not be easy. Dirk had his work cut out for him.

"Maral stag," he said, gesturing toward where the bull had been, "big." His movements indicated the size of the bull and the size of his horns. Using his fingers he demonstrated that the bull had six points on either side.

Tole and Deema understood.

"Maral stag," he said again. "No." He demonstrated no by waving his hands in a crisscrossing fashion in front of him. "No for Dirk. Maral stag no for Dirk." He ended the animated sentence pointing at himself.

He looked at me for help.

"How can I tell these Russian hunters that while the bull was a trophy in every sense of the word, that I just couldn't shoot him? I don't even know why myself. How can I explain it to them? I've taken smaller bulls. I've taken bigger bulls. What I want to explain to them is that the kill is not as important as the hunt. It never is. The thrill of being in this Siberian forest with friends that only a few short years ago were considered our enemies... the fun and excitement that we all shared finding the bull and stalking him... the look of wonder on the faces of Deema and Tole as they heard elk cows talk for the first time. That, Jake, was the hunt. The kill seemed so unimportant."

I understood. The mountain man was a true woodsman and hunter. More important, he was a teacher.

I shrugged my shoulders. "You're on your own, pal," was all I could offer.

"Kill," Dirk said over and over as he acted out the killing of a Maral stag. Then crisscrossing his hands as he said "not."

Dirk then began acting out the part of a hunter as he said the word "hunt." "Kill not hunt. Kill not hunt," he repeated.

Deema and Tole finally understood the message but they looked confused. After all, wasn't the purpose of the hunt to kill the game?

Dirk continued. "Hunt is hunt. Not kill." He patiently acted out each word.

Deema grasped the idea first and explained it to Tole. Tole still seemed confused.

"Hunt stored in memory. Dirk remember hunt forever." His gestures included pointing toward his brain many times as he repeated his statements.

In their faces I could see their understanding. In their eyes I could sense their respect for the hunter who stood before them.

"Dirk remember Deema and Tole forever," he continued his Oscar-winning performance.

Deema spoke in Russian again to Tole.

Tole nodded his head in complete understanding and said, "Aaah."

Without warning I was being hugged and kissed on each cheek by Deema while Tole was doing the same to Dirk. Then they traded places and as Tole was kissing me three times I felt a tear roll down my cheek. The mountain man was misty eyed too.

"Look around you, Dirk," I said. "This is the same country and these are the same men we've been taught to fear all our lives."

"Seems ridiculous, don't it, Jake," was his only reply.

That was the Dirk Ross I knew. Strong as an ox. Tough as a boot. Gentle as a lamb. He was who he was... totally authentic.

On our way back from Siberia we had an overnight layover in New York. I noticed one of the "think tank" places that had become so popular. It was my second experience, my first being a couple of years prior. The contraption was a cylinder filled with warm saltwater. When in the tank a person would lie in the saltwater on his back and relax. There in the quiet dark a person supposedly could get in touch with his higher self. I crawled into the tank with one thought in mind. I totally relaxed and asked the question, "Who or what am I supposed to follow?" As I floated in the water in a relaxed state, somewhere between sleep and not quite conscious, a sound began in my lower gut and began to rumble through my body and into my voice box. The sound was like someone talking underwater, a true guttural sound. I opened my mouth and it rumbled out through my lips, into the quiet darkness of the tank.

"FOLLOWLOVE...
F O L L O W L O V E...
F O L L O W L O V E"

While the sound was garbled, the message was loud and clear. It was as if someone else was speaking it through my body. It was a totally amazing experience. I finally had been given my answer. It was a simple message and easy to understand. I knew I would follow love for the rest of my life. Daddy had made it so simple for me.

"God is love" was his favorite verse of scriptures.

Following love is following God's path. It was as simple as that.

As soon as I could get to a phone I called Jeni and told her about my experience. She decided to fly to Durango and meet me that weekend. It was wonderful. We were in my travel trailer and it was cold. The temperature was 10 degrees at night. We talked for hours. We made love. We talked some more. We never had any trouble at all communicating. She was so interesting to visit with, and, more than that, so insightful. She always listened intently and offered suggestions that were equally insightful.

Chapter 9

"Life is either a daring adventure or nothing."
Helen Keller

JENI FINISHED HER undergraduate degree and moved to the Durango area to be with me. It was wonderful having her with me. She stayed with me in the RV for a couple of weeks. I was totally content to live there with her. She was not. She rented a beautiful little house in the foothills and allowed me to move in with her. It was perfect. She took a job working with developmentally delayed people and I continued selling real estate on the mountain. In the evenings I wrote my first novel, *Coogan*, which was an 1860s epic. I worked myself out of a job by selling all the units the owner of the mountain had available.

In the summer of 1993 I moved my travel trailer to Five Branches, a beautiful spot on the banks of Lake Vallecito. There in a little cabin called Outlaw West, Colt, like Dirk before him, staged trail rides and offered a hunting and fishing guide service. Colt and I spent the summer scouting new areas and new mountain ranges. We could leave at dawn and come back well after dark to find Jamie and Jeni preparing dinner for us. Sometimes we would ride and sometimes we would walk. By the end of the summer we were toughened to walking in the mountains. I knew that I was a real mountain man. I could keep up with Colt Ross, some twenty-seven years my junior.

Colt and I had some wonderful experiences together in the mountains. We loved to watch the birthing of the deer and elk calves and peek, from a distance, at the newborn bear cubs. We also got a bang out of sneaking up on game and tried every technique in the book that would allow us to get closer to them. Walking bent over and talking cow talk, we walked right through a meadow filled with elk and mulies. They looked at us but never ran. We were like two little kids... giddy over the experience. We laughed and told the story over and over.

Sometimes Jeni would ride into the mountains with me. Once, while riding on a particular trail, I suggested we take a cross-country journey and see if we could meet up with another trail I had in mind. We rode into an area with boggy soil that seemed to get boggier the farther we went. I urged my horse, a black gelding, down a fairly steep area while Jeni waited to see if it was safe. The gelding fell and rolled completely over me once while I struggled to get out of the saddle. I had a bruise where the saddle horn had pushed on my stomach as the horse and I tumbled down the slope. I knew I was lucky that day. I could have broken a leg or even worse.

Jeni had planned to continue her education in Colorado. She found, however, that the master's program in counseling she had planned to attend at Fort Lewis College started every three years. It was six months underway when she discovered that fact. It was determined for us; we would move back to the Dallas area where she could continue her dream of getting a master's degree in counseling.

Before we moved, however, 1994 started with a bang. Jaylie Lyn Ross was born. She was a beautiful baby and a scrapper. Jaylie came into the new year fighting. Papa Jake had a difficult time watching her fight when they had to put tubes into her lungs. Jamie and Colt were the proud parents of a baby girl.

I moved back to the Dallas area to be with Jeni. She enrolled in a program that allowed her to work during the day and go to school at night.

We lived in our travel trailer for several months before purchasing a home in McKinney. It did not matter to me where we lived. It did to

Jeni. I could live anywhere as long as Jeni was close by. I was following love. I would follow it wherever it led.

Jeni Darlin'

Her smile warms the coldest room
And melts my icy stress
Her infectious laugh
Takes away my sorrow
Her love enfolds me
Blanketing me in the essence of her being
Her body... so young and strong and perfect
Reminds me constantly that the little girl is all woman
She carried the key that unlocked my heart
And released the real man within
Her soul invited mine to unite and we became one
One being united in God's delicious love
The woman, little girl, mother, friend, lover and companion of which I speak
Is the one I call "Jeni Darlin'"
And the one I plan to, one day soon
Call my wife.

I love you, Jeni Darlin'

In 1994 Jeni's father died in San Antonio while she was visiting him. It was a sad time and very difficult for her. She was strong for her family and I was strong for her. We worked through the grieving process together. I was very glad I had expressed my love for his daughter to him before his death.

Colt and I went on a caribou hunt in 1995 into the backcountry of Quebec, Canada. It was a great trip filled with new experiences. You have never lived until you have flown into hunting and fishing camps by pontoon plane. Colt would "white knuckle" every time we were in the air. Tough as he was, he just did not like to be in the air.

On September 24, 1995, Jeni and I were married on the banks of the Vallecito River in a truly private and romantic ceremony. I first found the site many years earlier while roaming the country on horseback and had never forgotten about it. When I took Jeni there years later we were both overcome with emotion. It was truly a magical place and the site we felt was perfect for our wedding.

The site had been the inspiration for an earlier marriage in a mainstream novel I had written called *Coogan*. In that book I wrote of the wedding between Coogan and Jenny. Excerpts from that 1860s wedding went like this:

"Jenny, look around us. This is the place God made. We've been in cities before. That's what man made and he sometimes made a mess of things. But look around us. All we see is beauty. The quakies have even changed to a golden color for us. The sounds of the stream, the warmth of the sun, the birds singing. It's all perfect. *This* is real. *This* is what life is all about."

A mysterious puff of wind caused the quakies to shed a few of their golden leaves and some landed in Jenny's hair. She stood straight and confident... confident with her man. She faced him, looking into his eyes, and she could see the love there. She was purposefully quiet, breathing the moment, taking it into her lungs, allowing it to penetrate her being.

Coogan continued almost in a whisper, "Jenny, I bought this ring for you some fifteen years ago. I kept it with me all these years even though I knew you were married to someone else. I just couldn't bear to part with it. It belongs to you. I'd like to give it to you now as a symbol of my love for you. I reckon I'd like to marry you right here, now. Unashamed as we both are, in the forest that we both love so much. Here where God made everything and everything is in its special place. You and I stand together... without anything... but with everything."

Jenny felt sensations she had never experienced before. They were overwhelming.

Coogan continued, "I give you this ring, Jenny, as a token of my love for you, and as the circle of the ring never ends, neither will my love for you. I'll not ask anything of you, Jenny. I'll not promise you anything either. Promises are obligations and I don't feel like my love for you is an obligation. It is not a responsibility. It's much more than that. It's too real to be controlled by anything other than what it is."

Jenny could see the tears welling in Coogan's eyes and felt those in her own. Coogan looked deeply into her eyes now. All the way to her soul. She was exposed. There was nothing to hide behind, and strangely enough she didn't want to hide. She could sense his vulnerability. She could sense his weaknesses which, in essence, were his very strengths.

He whispered, "Jenny, in the sight of God and all his magnificence, I give you this ring as a token of my love and devotion to you. I have loved you forever, even before I can remember meeting you. I looked for you. I found you. I lost you. But I never stopped loving you and I never will. We can get married in a church if you want to, but Jenny, I'll tell you this. For me there will never be another ceremony as meaningful as this one. The trees, the squirrels, and the birds and the deer are our witnesses as I slip this ring on your finger and say, 'With this ring, I thee wed.' God put us here to be together. No man can ever change that. I love you, Jenny. And if you'll have me, I'm now your husband."

Jenny stood there. Her senses were reeling. It seemed that everything in the world had stopped. She looked at Coogan. Tears were rolling down his cheeks.

She was aware of the trees. She could feel the gentle wind caressing her skin. She could hear the birds. They were all watching her. The leaves were falling all around her and she was spinning in a beautiful dreamlike setting. The green of the forest... the blue of the sky... the golden of the quakies... and Coogan, the man she loved, in the center of it all. He placed the ring on her finger and she looked at it, then back into his eyes. She wanted to speak, but there were no words. She melted into the moment.

Finally she spoke in a whisper as tears of joy rolled down her cheeks, "Coogan, you are the only man I've ever loved. You are the man I used to see in my dreams. We had obstacles to overcome. We had a bridge to build and a river to cross. You are the man God put here for me. Like the trees we will grow strong together. We will not shade the other but allow it to grow its own way and we will stand together side by side in the knowledge that we are independent of each other but tied together in a bond of God's love and our love for each other. Our roots will grow deep, deep into the very essence of God's love and we will survive every obstacle together and learn through these periods. Coogan, I am marrying you, and with the forest as my witness I pledge nothing to you but myself and my love, which is all I have to give. I love you, Coogan. You are now my husband. You have been always."

He held her then. Unashamed, they let the emotions and feelings overtake them. Later they would marry in a church. Later they would marry for man. Today they married for themselves. Today they fulfilled their destiny. They knew it and the living forest around them knew it.

The birds sang. The squirrels chattered while the stream bubbled its happiness. A doe and her three fawns moved closer to them, seemingly aware of the special event that had just taken place. The wind and leaves danced for them. They were home.

My vows on our wedding went much like the vows Coogan gave to his Jenny. It was filled with emotion and love. Something very special happened on our wedding day.

Right after we said our vows and kissed, a movement caused us to look on the ridge just above our location on the river. What we saw there was very special. Our wedding ceremony had been witnessed by four very special visitors: a doe and her three fawns. It was surreal to have written it in the book earlier and have it happen later. Jeni and I knew that our marriage had been blessed by someone more powerful than the universe itself.

Chapter 10

"We make a living by what we get, we make a life by what we give."

Winston Churchill

ONE MONTH AFTER our wedding I was pulling into a Dallas restaurant parking place with Jeni. It was lunch time. Just as we were getting out of the car my cell phone rang; it was my secretary. She asked to speak to Jeni. I thought it a bit odd. When Jeni hung up the phone, she looked at me and said slowly, "Jake, there was a plane crash. Dirk and Colt were both killed."

Tears flew from my eyes and I began to sob. I tried to talk. I tried to understand but my emotions overtook me. My two best friends in the world were now dead. The two men I had hunted with for years were gone. As fast as the blink of an eye, two of the finest men in the world lost their lives. One was my son-in-law. The other, my best friend.

Jeni held me. Right there in the parking lot we sobbed together. She shared my sorrow. She knew how much the boys meant to me and instinctively she knew my feelings. There was no talking. Words were not needed.

My thoughts turned to Jamie. How was she taking it? I pulled myself together enough to make the call. She screamed when she heard my voice. I tried to be strong for her, but it was difficult.

"I'll be there as soon as I can," I told her.

Jeni and I talked little as we packed. I knew Jeni would have to return to Dallas after the funeral, and she knew that I would have to stay. That was just the way it was. Colt was an outfitter, and hunting season was scheduled to begin in four days. He had thirty-five hunters booked on the first hunt. We would all just have to pull together and guide the elk hunters even though our hearts were somewhere else. I would have plenty of help. All the Ross brothers would pitch in. I knew that.

"I have to be with her. I have to go. Jamie needs me," I whispered. "What a tragedy. Jaida is only one month old and Jaylie isn't even two yet. Neither little girl will get to know how wonderful their daddy is... and Dirk's five kids... and the boys' parents. How will they cope?" I began to sob all over again.

And Jeni was there to comfort me... to listen... and to share my sorrow.

We left in the middle of the afternoon and knew we would drive all night. We arrived at Jamie's the next morning after a fourteen-hour drive. Everything was chaotic and it seemed like a nightmare to me. Jamie needed my fatherly strength and I mustered all I could and gave it to her. Jackie came by plane and helped with the girls. She was a total blessing to Jamie during that period. I did what I could to help her with the arrangements, working with the parents of Colt and Dirk who were totally grief-stricken. Even in their grief, the Ross family stood together like the Rock of Gibralter.

I took a morning to go to the site of the plane crash with a video camera to try to record anything that might be significant. It was a tragic sight. Bits and pieces of the plane lay all over the ground and in trees around. The ground was scorched where the plane had gone in upside down after first hitting a tree. The picture became clear to me as I saw the bits and pieces of debris lying everywhere. I could see where the wing clipped a tall pine and where the plane turned over. I found bits of the cockpit up in the trees. It was eerie being there alone, but I found myself wanting to stay on that mountain. I did not know why. My best friends had died there. I wanted to spend time there, but I knew I couldn't. Jamie needed my strength and support.

The funeral arrangements were complicated by the fact that thirty-five elk hunters had booked and were on their way in to hunt. It was decided that Jon Ross, father of the boys and the patriarch of the family, would run the hunts. I would handle the money and the books, and we would do our best to get through the hunting season. It was a difficult time. Horses had to be shuffled. Camps had to be set. Food had to be packed in. Wood had to be cut. Last-minute details had to be tended to. Fortunately, Jon and the five brothers knew what to do and enlisted the help of other friends of the family to help out. We would go from the funeral home to Jamie's house to the trailhead several times a day. I was there, taking charge where I could be helpful and letting others use their talents where they could help. There were a lot of people helping. Those two boys and their families were blessed with friends.

The Mormon church in Bayfield was overflowing with friends and relatives the day of the funeral. I was asked to give the eulogy for Colt. I mustered all my strength and gave my part without a single breakdown. It was one of the most difficult things I had ever done. Dirk and Colt were my best friends. More like brothers. I loved them so.

Right after the graveside ceremony we all took off our suits and ties, put on our blue jeans, and grabbed our saddles. That very afternoon we started packing hunters into the several camps already erected in the San Juan National Forest. The closest camp was a three-hour horseback ride. I assigned myself to the Willow Camp, which was in the Weminuche Wilderness and six hours by horse from the trailhead.

The first day of the hunt I took a doctor into a remote area where I had seen tons of elk in the past. We started at 9,000 feet and climbed on foot to 12,500 feet. I don't know why I kept moving; I just could not be still. I had to walk. The doctor was tough but he was plenty tired. I had no earthly idea what time it was until all of a sudden it was dark. Suddenly it dawned on me that we were miles from camp and from the nearest trail down the mountain. I was prepared to spend the night on the mountain, but the doctor insisted on going back to the camp. That was okay with me. I still had tons of energy. Little did I know that I was in the grieving process. I started down the mountain at a good clip. The doctor was dragging behind and I had to wait for him as he stumbled and fell down the steep mountain in the dark.

After a few hours I found a trail that I knew would make the walk much easier. While it switched back and forth on the steep slope, it was much easier than going straight down the side of the mountain.

My daughter was weighing heavy on my heart and I could feel her calling me as we walked down the mountain trail. She needed me, and the last place I wanted to be was in the hunting camp. There were plenty of guides for the hunters and a good cook, so as soon as we made camp I helped the doctor get some food and listened to him tell the story of how mountain man Jake had nearly killed him on that mountain.

I said my goodbyes and hopped on a molly mule for the long ride down the mountain. That old mule did not want to leave that camp, and she and I had to have a heart-to-heart discussion. While she was bucking me I was hanging on, determined that I was in command. As it turned out, I was. It took quite a bit of convincing but the mule and I finally made it down the ten miles to the trailhead. I was in no mood to put up with a mule telling me what I was or was not going to do.

I checked in on Jamie and we cried together again for a long time. Later I sat propped up next to a one-hundred-foot tall pine tree and wrote two poems. One about my friend Dirk and one about my friend Colt.

My Friend

I met him in the late seventies, the man from the mountains
Through the years we became friends… close friends
Riding the trail… climbing the peaks… following the elk… touching the stars
Sharing our lives, our secrets, our hopes, our dreams, our fears
Spinning yarns… laughing… crying
A real man was he, the man from the mountains
A paradox… tough and at the same time tender… strong and gentle
Honest, dependable, hard working, friendly, a real family man

An encourager, a giver, a lover of life best describe him
　　Around the world we traveled together, that mountain man and me
From the San Juan Weminuche to the Siberian tundra
　　Up and down mountains too steep, across streams too swift
Into places we should never have gone… blazing new trails
　　Sharing each adventure and I thank God for giving me those days
Those hours… those minutes… those moments when we were together
　　The mountain man was and will always be my friend.
I love you, Dirk Ross.

　　Jake

Colt

He followed us around, me and Dirk, mostly Dirk
　　And we watched him grow
Full of life and love and with a million-dollar smile
　　Before our eyes he became a man… a mountain man
Always smiling, always happy, always willing was Colt
　　He was tough, strong, honest and kind
Mostly Colt was genuine, the kind of man
　　That another man would respect and they did
I remember telling my daughter about him
　　About how he was a *real* man
Smart girl she was, she married him
　　Wonderful thing for a man to pick his own son-in-law
What a blessing to have known him, to have loved him
　　To have him father my grandchildren
What a gift to have known Colt Ross, the boy… the man
　　How delicious to have had him as my friend
How special to have ridden the trail, to have climbed
　　The mountains and touched the sky
With a man so unquestionably authentic
　　I love you, Colt Ross!

　　Jake

Times were difficult for Jamie, and I knew that she would need help if she was ever going to make it through this tough time. Jackie and I both wanted to help our daughter. This was a labor of love for us. While Jackie left her job in Dallas and moved to be with Jamie and help her with the girls, I left my job with Cushman and Wakefield and also moved into the area to take over the outfitting business. I once again moved into a travel trailer. I had sold mine when I bought the home in Dallas. It was decided that Jeni would come later after she finished her master's degree in May of 1996.

Jamie was the owner of forty-two horses and mules and a business that had been good for her and Colt. As I figured it, the assets of the company would bring, at most, about $50,000. After thoroughly considering and then writing down the strengths and weaknesses of the business, I assessed the situation from the perspective that maybe I could run the business and sell it as a company. I looked at the cash flow and decided that, with proper management, the little business could be worth quite a bit of money. Then I assessed my strengths and weaknesses from the standpoint of running such a business. On the plus side, I was a hunter who knew the area. I knew animals and how to care for them. I knew how to work. On the minus side I knew that this was a massive undertaking for anyone, especially a fifty-five-year-old. I analyzed the deal alright, but what really made the decision for me was that my daughter needed me. I was going to help her. I made the decision that I would run the business for Jamie and bring it into the current decade with computer-driven databases, contracts, and cash flow analysis.

I knew the task would be difficult. Aside from the fact that I was taking on a huge physical undertaking at age fifty-five, I also knew that I would have to rebuild the business from the ground up. I figured that hunters who had hunted with Dirk and Colt would probably not be willing to book again until they knew what the new outfit was about. I was right. I spent the spring booking hunters for the next season and the summer running trail rides and getting horses and equipment in shape for the upcoming hunting season. I hired people, fired people, wrote contracts and menus, and, in general, took on the job of general manager of the business.

I had one objective: to sell the business to an all-cash buyer at a price that would take care of Jamie and the girls. Other objectives included bringing the business into the '90s with computer-based management programs, increasing the cash flow, and operating the business for a couple of years at a net profit that could be duplicated by a buyer that was willing to work the business.

More than one person told me I was doomed to failure from the start. I never believed that for one second. I was also told that being an outfitter was a young man's business and at fifty-five, I did not stand a chance. It seems all my life I've been told that I was too something. Too young, too old, too clumsy, too slow, too tall. There was always something. If a person believes what he is told, it is true. I guess I believed in me and my own abilities more than anyone else did. I just smiled and went on about my business. It was a formidable challenge but I had always loved a challenge.

It was a difficult time financially for Jeni and me. I did not want to take any money for running the outfitting business. I had to take enough to live on, but that was all. The rest went to Jamie and the girls.

There was plenty to do. There was the physical part of the summer trail rides. There was taking care of the horses and mules, which included worming, feeding, and shoeing. My animal husbandry background came in handy here. There was putting the tack and equipment in order and keeping it in order. There was inventory. There were contracts to write. There were bank lines of credit that had to be established. There was the hiring of key employees. There was the constant maintenance. In addition, there was the mental anguish as I watched my daughter deal with the loss of her husband and as I dealt with my own loss of my two best friends. Most of all, there was being away from Jeni. Just married and separated by a tragedy. It was extremely difficult.

About 1:00 A.M. one night I was doing some repairs to our riding stable, which required the use of an electric drill. Some metal shavings went into my eye and I had to drive sixty miles with one eye to the Durango hospital. I had no idea that a metal shaving in the eye could cause that much pain, but let me tell you, it hurt like hell. The doctors put one drop of something in my eye and removed the shaving, but I learned a very valuable lesson about drilling — always use safety glasses. I learned a lot of lessons being an outfitter, not the least of which is that I never want to do it again.

My fatherly duties took me into an area I really did not want to be in — legal battles. I have always respected others and expected others to do the right thing. Occasionally though, because we are people, we disagree on what is right and what is not.

Colt and Dirk had chartered the plane and pilot from Durango Air Service in Durango, Colorado, and when the National Transportation Safety Board published their findings it appeared to me that there was negligence. I interviewed a couple of attorneys and recommended one to Jamie. If there was any negligence we would attempt to find it. This was terribly unpleasant for me, as Colt and Dirk's parents were against the hiring of an attorney no matter what. But we did what we had to do. Jamie and Crystal, Dirk's wife, hired the same aviation attorney to investigate further. At his request we hired an expert to sift through the wreckage and investigate the plane itself.

"What do you mean the insurance company won't let him look at the wreckage? Don't they have to?" I asked the attorney incredulously.

"Oh, we will eventually get to see the plane, alright," Bruce stated. "But insurance companies can be real hard to deal with if they want to and this one seems to want to."

Apparently, when there is a plane crash the remains of the plane are taken to a place that is controlled by the owner's insurance company. That plane's remains sat in a snow-covered lot for close to a year before our expert was even allowed to inspect them, and that was only after a lot of legal haggling. When he finally was granted the right to view the aircraft, he found that the carburetor was missing.

"What do you mean the carburetor is missing? Where is it?" I asked.

"We don't know where it is. The plane has been sitting there a long time," was the answer.

"Well, isn't the carburetor a key piece of evidence in this case?"

"Not if we can't find it."

"So let me get this straight. For over a year the insurance company would not let us see the plane and now the carburetor is missing. Is that correct?"

"That is correct."

"And there is nothing we can do about it."

"That is correct. Unless we can find it and prove that someone took it with some malicious intent."

"Boy, all this seems to have an odor about it, don't you think?" I kept pushing but it did me absolutely no good whatsoever.

We were at the mercy of the insurance company, which either did not want to accept liability on a claim or legitimately thought they did not owe it. A key and critical part of the aircraft was missing, never to be seen or heard of again. Go figure. My daughter, granddaughters, and best friend's family were at the mercy of the attorneys. I was appalled that anyone would not want to help the widows and orphans. Not only did they not want to help, they wanted to keep anyone else from helping them. I wished I could talk to them myself but that was not allowed either. There were some questions I wanted to ask and some answers I was sure I could get one way or the other. I was disgusted with the system.

Trouble was coming at me from a number of levels — attorneys, lawsuits, horses and mules, employees, grief, emotional trauma, and the death of two best friends. The worst part of it all was being away from the girl I loved while she was finishing her degree. I was plenty glad she was studying to be a counselor because I was pretty sure I was going to need one. People asked me how, with all the pressures on me, I could keep such a positive attitude and always have a smile on my face. Well, the answer was simple: I didn't. My telephone conversations with Jeni helped keep me focused as did going into the woods and screaming as loud as I could. Still, I never once thought that the objective would not be reached. I knew, no matter how tough things became, that in the end everything would work out the way it was supposed to. My faith in God kept me steadfast in that thought.

On a regular basis I had been talking to an attorney friend of the Ross family named Jack Bloise. Not only was he an attorney, Jack was an adventurer, a hunter, and an ex-Navy SEAL. Jack wanted to buy Rocky Mountain Outfitters but had no money. He said that he could run the business and do a "payout" with the profits. His plan made sense to him but not to me. My daughter needed cold, hard cash. When I would not consider that proposal, Jack proposed something else. He would help run the business for a year. I wasn't too keen on the idea because Jack was not a known entity in the field of outfitting hunters. Couple that with the fact that Jack was from the north, and I could see some real problems.

He had several qualities I really liked, however. One was I knew that he was plenty tough. You are not a Navy SEAL without toughness. Two, the boy had perseverance and that impressed me the most. He really wanted to become an outfitter. Three, Jack was plenty smart. I figured what he did not know he could learn.

"Jack, I plan to hire an operations manager for RMO," I explained on the phone. "That person will be fully in charge of the day-to-day operations of the company. I will handle all the booking, the contracts, the paperwork, and the operations manager will handle the wranglers, cooks, getting the people in and out of the camps, etc. I will be responsible for seeing to it that the animals have the right nutrition, the hunters and fisherman are fed well, that there is enough money to make payroll. The operations manager will report to me and to me only. I will help him as much as I can, but he will have to gain the respect of the people that report to him. Now here is the problem as I see it. I will already have hired the staff that will report to you. That is not fair to you. Not that you won't be able to fire them because you will. You can also hire others, but, my friend, it will be an uphill battle because there are some I have already hired that have worked for Colt or Dirk in the past and they will be jealous of your position. Next, you don't know enough about the business or the equipment to set it up properly. I have some real reservations about putting you in that position."

"I can handle all that," Jack assured me.

"I don't know. You will have to move your wife here. What does she think of all this?"

"She isn't too happy about it, but she will come with me. She is pregnant, you know."

"Congratulations, Jack. There is nothing like a baby. When is she due?" I asked, mentally raising a red flag.

"Late summer, but it won't affect me in the hunting season. She will just have to be okay with it."

"Jack, do you think that is fair to her?"

"We can handle it. Don't worry about her."

I took all these factors into account before I made a decision. Actually his persistence made the decision for me. I figured that anyone who wanted that job that bad would find a way to be good at it. He certainly had the "want to" factor going for him.

Jack could not move into the area until June. I knew this would be tough for him because he would have to begin supervising a crew that I hired. Our summer trail rides opened on May 15 and I needed a full working crew in place well before that time. It was not the best of circumstances for Jack. I would hire and train the employees that he would be expected to supervise. I hoped he could handle it.

Jeni received her master's degree on May 10 and we celebrated by packing up and moving her to the area to be with me. We left our furniture in our house in McKinney and just took off, hoping our house would rent while we were gone. I moved Jeni into an RV near the outfitting business and we stayed there until June 1 when we bought another RV to live in.

What a honeymoon we had. Maybe I should rephrase it sarcastically. It was just a totally glorious honeymoon for us. Rushing... moving from our home into an RV... shoveling horse manure. Jeni was determined that she would help me any way she could. That too would be an interesting situation. Cowboys and wranglers don't much like having a woman telling them what to do. Looking back on it all, I'm surprised she came.

Together we started cleaning up Outlaw West Livery, which was a roughly built cabin where we began all our trail rides. I pretty much had all the horses and mules shod by that time and we began cleaning up the livery and bringing our tack out of storage and into the tack sheds we had built for the purpose. Jeni was a human dynamo. She cleaned everything, and it needed it.

I had hired some wranglers who knew the trails and some we had to teach the trails to. Everything was working pretty well. We saddled horses in the morning, unsaddled them in the evening, and made sure the wranglers were well fed. Things started pretty slow and that was just fine with us. The mountain trails were still pretty muddy. Jeni, just out of grad school, was shoveling horse manure. We were definitely on top of the world.

By the time June rolled around and Jack and his wife made it to our area, we were in full swing. All the wranglers knew he was coming and that he would be their boss. It would be up to Jack to build his own relationships with the wranglers. He had his share of problems but, all in all, he did a good job. Tough as he was, he bought a little mule that was tougher. Many a night his mule and the pack string showed up at Outlaw West before he did. I was always worried about him. I guess I shouldn't have been.

Our operating plan was broken down by categories. We had summer trail rides and day trips, drop camps, semi-guided trips, full-service trips, and lodge facilities. We operated our trail rides from May 15 through Labor Day weekend. Our trail rides were in some of the most beautiful country in the world. The San Juan National Forest is gorgeous. We took people on rides ranging from one or two hours up to half day or full day rides. In addition, we offered breakfast rides and dinner rides. On both rides the trail climbed well above Lake Vallecito and offered views so breathtakingly beautiful it was difficult to tear people away. Then it was on to a high mountain meadow where a cook prepared either breakfast of pancakes, sausage, eggs, bacon, and toast, or dinner consisting of steaks and chicken cooked to order over a grill. At these we sang and I often recited one of my famous Jakespearian poems, such as "No Name Mule on Elk Point Run."

> I bought her from a good ol' boy
>   Texas he was from
> The biggest mule I ever see'd
>   To me she now had come

Prouder than proud I was of her
    When I saddled her all pretty like
My back was to her a' talkin' to them dudes
    When she reached over and gave me a bite

Not a good place to be bit by a mule
    Especially when you're all washed up and shiny
And that old mule she just picked the spot
    And bit me right on my hiney

I climbed in the saddle a little sore
    Couldn't wait to ride the Elk Point Run
Leadin' all them dudes on that molly mule
    We was a' fixin' to have some fun

That mule and I would lead them up and down
    And all around as well
Though steep so steep they'd close their eyes and pray
    Like an evangelist in hell

They watched as we started up the trail
    My mule without a name
They saw her crow hop a little bit
    And saw me pull her mane

We left the lodge and I was proud
    And nameless was a' doin' alright
Steppin' out strong and fine
    Of a sudden she stopped to take a bite

I was a' lookin' back at the time
    And that was a big mistake
Cause the limb that took my hat and punched my eye
    Also caused that mule to break

She took off like a bat out of hell
    With me yellin' "Whoa"
A' holdin' on to that saddle horn
    And a' hopin' she would slow

Then she commenced to buckin'
    And I thought I'd ridden them all
But that old mule came unglued
    And I commenced my fall

I hung on for eight seconds
    Of that I was sure

But what that saddle horn was a' hittin' when she bucked
    Made me feel very insecure

Now I'd been throwed before
    In rodeos and such
But let me tell you now
    It ain't never hurt so much

Them rodeos have soft sand
    And I was a' prayin' for that kind of landing
But that old rock up on the run
    Must have figured my butt needed branding

I wish I could say it got some better
    And them dudes didn't help none
Some was a' grinnin' and some was a' laughin'
    And I wasn't havin' no fun

After 'twas over I sat in a stream
    Certain parts was a hurtin' and I wanted to scream
I wondered what happened to my baritone voice
    Now I was a' talkin' in a high squeaky voice

Well, that's the story and I'm sorry to say
    That on my no-name mule on the Elk Point Run
It was one hell of a day.

We had five different U.S. Forest Service permitted camps. Three of those were in the Weminuche Wilderness, where nothing motorized of any kind was allowed. That meant that wood had to be cut by hand; no chainsaws were allowed at these camps.

I gave job descriptions to each employee and went over them in detail. They had to sign the job description. They were definitive job descriptions with requirements that had to be met. This was a business and I wanted it to be run like a business. In addition to the responsibilities of each employee, I set up procedures and safety checks for the employees to follow. We went over these procedures in detail and they included grooming, saddling, bridling, and removing the saddle.

We had weekly operations meetings with a written agenda. We had a standard orientation for guests where we explained the basics of horses, tack, and rules such as checking cinches and no trotting toward the corral. Basically we taught our clients riding skills whether they planned to ride for one hour or ten days. We wanted them to have a good experience and we wanted our animals to have a good experience also.

I drew up a full business plan, complete with mission statement and objectives. Included were horse rental agreements, release of liability agreements, fully guided and semi-guided hunting agreements, medical and physical condition forms, pack trip agreements. I wanted our clients to know what they were getting into, what we expected of them, and what they could expect of us.

Jeni drew up camp menus and staff menus, and worked with the cooks of all our camps. She pitched in anywhere she was needed and did anything required plus tons of stuff not required.

The first time I took her on a long trip into the mountains was interesting. We needed to check on a camp on the Pine River in the Weminuche. It would take us five to six hours to ride in. That also means five or six hours to ride out. Makes for a long day. Our packer, Brady, was going with us as we needed to take some supplies to the camp. Jeni wanted to go because we had booked five adult couples on a fishing and sightseeing trip into the wilderness the next week. She had volunteered to cook at that camp. We needed to make sure wood was cut and Jeni wanted to familiarize herself with the wood-burning stove she would be cooking on.

I was totally excited because Jeni had never seen anything as spectacular as the country we were packing in to. I put her on a little molly mule that was surefooted and a great ride. Jeni was not an accomplished rider but she was certainly game.

The trip in was uneventful and she loved riding in, but I could tell she was a bit tired. The climb wasn't difficult for the animals as we went from about 7,500 feet to 10,000 feet, and the view was spectacular. Basically we rode along the Pine River, but we saw waterfalls, beaver ponds, and game along the way. She fell in love with the camp, and when I showed her a 1000-foot waterfall she was hooked.

At 10,000 feet the stars are really bright and you can just almost reach out and touch them. I had hoped for that kind of ride down the mountain. What I got instead was a totally black night and drizzling rain. We started back about 6:00 P.M., and by 7:30 it was so dark I could not even see my hand in front of my face six inches away. I had Brady in the lead with the four pack mules behind him, then Jeni, and I was bringing up the rear. I could not see her. I could barely hear her when I tried to talk because of the rain. I thought, "Oh, no. She will never come back again." How wrong I was.

We rode into the trailhead about 2:00 A.M. and Jeni was so excited.

"That was incredible!" She was talking ninety words a second. "I rode in the rain. I rode at night. It was pitch black. I am so proud of myself. Thank you, Jake, for letting me do this. I am so happy. Tired, but happy. I was scared to death. Scared to death. I was thinking, where am I? Where is Jake? Is he still behind me? Where is Brady? Oh, my God, I was so scared. But, I did it. I overcame my fear. I feel so good. I did it, didn't I?"

There I was thinking that she must have been having a miserable time and she was enjoying every second of it.

I smiled and shook my head. "You did it, Jeni darlin'. You did it."

I hugged her then and thought, "She reminds me of a female character in one of Louis L'Amour's westerns. This is a lady to ride the river with."

Everything Jeni did made me love her just that much more. Here she was, completely out of her element and far away from her family. I had taken her from our comfortable home on the golf course in McKinney and put her in a travel trailer, for heaven's sake. We were taking it on the chin financially, and Jeni was in there every day helping me help my daughter, and making the most of it all. She seemed to look on everything as a new adventure. She definitely was a lady to ride the river with.

She sat her mule comfortably when we took the couples back down the river. She was confident that she could cook and handle any chore that needed to be done, and I was pretty convinced she handle anything no matter what.

On the second night the wrangler and I had staked the horses out in a meadow about a half-mile downriver. Actually we only had to stake the lead mare. Where that little gray mare was, all the other horses and mules would stay. Horses in herds are that way. There is always a lead horse in any herd. The gray mare was our lead horse and we staked her out by putting a hobble on her left front ankle. The hobble was then tied to a stake in the middle of the meadow with a thirty-foot length of rope. This gave her a sixty-foot diameter area in which to graze. She would have plenty to eat.

The previous night I had rigged up a battery-operated fence around the cook tent where Jeni and I slept. I had to tell her what it was for — to keep the bears out. That didn't scare her very much. That wasn't the problem. It was the little critters that she didn't do well with. It was the field mice and the chipmunks. The minute we turned the lantern out they constantly ran into and out of the cook tent and sometimes across our beds. They didn't bother me, but they definitely bothered Jeni.

About midnight on the second night I had just fallen asleep when I felt this tugging on my sleeve.

"I can't do this anymore," she said as I turned to look at her.

"You can't do what?"

"I can't sleep in this tent with all these things running all over the place. One just ran across my pillow and I felt the fur touch my face."

"Oh, baby, it was probably just a little chipmunk."

"I don't care, I cannot sleep here anymore."

I thought for a minute. "Let's take our bedrolls outside into the meadow. It is a clear night and we can watch the stars. It will be romantic." Actually it was sounding better to me all the time.

She was up in a flash. We carried our sleeping bags outside and right into the middle of a little meadow. I zipped them together and taped our Thermarest sleeping pads together and we crawled into bed. It was crisp, cold, and beautiful. You could touch the stars. It was

very romantic and we both were euphoric. I saw a shooting star, then
another. Jeni saw a couple. We began to whisper. One thing led to
another and the mood was perfect.

We kissed, and just when things were beginning to heat up
Jeni said, "What's that? What's that noise?"
I listened to the rumble in the distance and knew immedi-
ately what it was. "Grab your clothes and run to the trees.
It's a stampede."

We both took off as quickly as we could and I pulled her behind
some trees just as the first horse flew by. Fifteen horses and mules
ran over our sleeping bags that night, but we were well hidden behind
the trees, trying to get dressed. The mare had somehow pulled the
stake up and was running along, slinging it on a thirty-foot rope. They
came through the camp first and into our meadow. After things settled
down a little, we checked to see if anyone was hurt and what damage
had been done. Only one tent was knocked down — the supply tent.
Our bedrolls were no worse for wear. It did take me a while to find one
of my boots though.

The wrangler and I caught the horses and staked them back out. I
couldn't get Jeni to sleep in the meadow that night, and whatever was
going on before the stampede was definitely over... all because of one
little old gray mare.

Chapter 11

"If a man does his best, what else is there?"
General George S. Patton

THE AIR WAS CRISP and clean and the June sun was peeking through the branches of the trees as I walked across the footbridge that crossed the steep, water-filled drainage. I took a moment to stop on the bridge and look down into the rushing water below. It had been a cold winter and the snow was still melting on the mountains, sending torrents of water down the drainage on its way into the river some thousand or so yards south of where I stood. My heart had been heavy since I had left my blue pickup at the Pine River trailhead and tugged my backpack into place. I had heard nothing but the peaceful sounds of the wind rustling through the trees, birds, and occasional squirrels chattering. Now the water was rushing over the rocks with such ferocity that it sounded like a freight train.

My pack was lighter than usual, probably no heavier than forty pounds. I crossed the bridge, made the familiar turn up the mountain, and spotted a log close to the raging torrent of water. I sat down, peeled my backpack off, and took a long, slow swig. I thought about the conversation Jeni and I had shared yesterday.

"I'm going to backpack into the Willow for a few days. Want to come with me?" I asked Jeni.

"I know that you just want some alone time. Am I right?"

"Not alone time, Jeni. I would love to have you come with me. I just need to clear my head and get a plan together. I figure if I take some time in the woods and carry my journal I can figure out what to do from here."

"You go ahead, baby, and take as long as you want. I understand."

She was like that. She never tried to talk me out of anything but let me do what I felt best. She knew my love of the mountains and nature and knew that I had some decisions to make that would have a profound effect on both our lives. She wanted to give me the space I needed to make those decisions. It was just one more thing I loved about Jeni.

RMO had a successful hunting season and most of the '96 hunters had already placed their deposits for the '97 hunt. We had been fortunate. Not only had it been a profitable year for RMO, we had only one minor injury to one hunter whose horse had unloaded him on a steep descent.

I laughed as I thought about the time I had been asleep on my mule as we were coming down a similar steep slope. I had been exhausted. My days in hunting camps started at 3:30 in the morning as I caught up and fed the horses, started warming fires near the hunters' tents, and prepared for the day. We left our camps before dawn and rode to the location where we would hunt for the day. I would try to catch a catnap, but they were few and far between. I generally crawled into my bedroll after midnight. It was a grueling ordeal to be an outfitter.

It had been well after dark when we had begun our descent down the mountain. Two of my hunters were in the lead and I was on a mule I trusted completely. I was dreaming. The dream I was in took me back to the days I had tried riding broncs in the rodeo. I dreamed I was being bucked. Only thing was, it wasn't a dream; I was being bucked. By the time I realized what was going on I was in the air and literally flipping over the horse in front of me. I landed on my butt to the left of the trail and near a pile of rocks. It spooked the horse that I had gone over, but the rider was competent and was able to control him. I had been lucky that night.

I thought about the mule train of five fully packed mules that had run over me and stepped on my head. Freaky accident. It had given me a slight concussion, but nothing major. I had been lucky.

The only other problem of any significance we'd had during the '96 season was when we lost one of the wranglers on a stormy night. Our hunters had followed his tracks to a swollen stream, but they did not come out the other side. We had a day or so of worry about the wrangler but found that he had gone down the mountain to be with his girlfriend. True love never sleeps.

All in all it had been a truly successful year, and a harsh one. The winter months had been plenty tough. We had six feet of snow one night. I had to plow the half-mile driveway to Jamie's house every couple of hours just to keep it open. Harder still was keeping the horses fed. Keeping the snow out of the corral was done by hand and the horses all but ran me over getting to the hay I threw out for them. It was the hardest work I had ever done. Cutting firewood, splitting it, hauling it. Feeding and plowing were everyday tasks for me. It was a winter for the books. Still, I stayed focused through it all. Focused on selling the business.

Jeni had found a great house for us to rent and we had moved our belongings out of the RV. For several months we were making two house payments until our house finally rented in McKinney.

I had presented the RMO business plan to a number of people who I felt could buy the business for all cash. We had done well and had exceeded the bullish income projections I had made when I took over the business. Armed with this "we did better than our projections" information, I pushed some of the people who had expressed an interest. It was hard for them to argue when I pointed out to them that if a real estate man from Texas could do it, think of what a person who understood the business could do. Not that I believed that for one second. Most people just don't want to work hard enough to get the job done. I doubted that anyone would do better, but I knew that if I operated the business another year it would do considerably better.

In April of 1997 we sold the business. The buyer wanted Jamie's home and the few acres she owned. I thought it was the proper decision because the old house was an "add-on" type of house and was in need of constant repair. Colt could have handled it. I could have handled it. Jamie and those two little girls had no business trying to handle it. She bought a brand new home in Durango that I thought way too big for her needs, but I wanted to see my daughter happy, so I said nothing.

I had completed my mission. My objective was complete and for that I was thankful. The problem was I had been so focused on helping Jamie that I totally forgot about Jeni's and my finances. We were busted. Worse, we had been living on our credit cards. Someone was living in our house in McKinney so we had no place to go until the lease ran out in December. Jeni and I wanted to stay in the Colorado area and I felt I could start up an outdoor video program. We were out of money. I tried to sell our house to our renter but he declined.

I was going into the woods to determine what my next course of action would be. Should we move back to Dallas or continue to live in the Durango area? I had my journal and pen with me and I planned to come out of the backwoods with a plan of action. It would start with where it always started... at the beginning. I would write the strengths and weaknesses Jeni and I now possessed and the strengths and weaknesses of each location. I would clarify my thoughts here. Jeni and I would make the decision together.

Two weeks ago I had hiked back to the spot where the plane had crashed on the mountain some two years ago, the spot where my two best friends had lost their lives. Something had drawn me back there like a magnet. What I found triggered all kinds of emotions that I had not been able to share with anyone, even Jeni.

"Maybe I can write the story here," I thought. "Maybe I can write about it now."

I climbed the faint trail that Dirk and I had carved out of the side of the mountain years before with an ax, shovel, and machete. It was so steep that we had to make over a hundred switchbacks. Only deer and elk could have gone straight up the mountain here, and certainly no horse or mule or man without a rope. It was steep where I was going, and I was certain I would see no one up there. Just the way I wanted it.

I loved being in the mountains. Maybe it was the solitude I craved. Maybe it was the beauty. John Muir, the great naturalist, had said it best when he said, "Going to the mountains is going home."

I was always amused at people's reactions when they learned I loved to go into the backwoods alone.

"Aren't you scared? Aren't you afraid a bear will get you?"

"I just enjoy the beauty of it all. The peace and quiet. Have you ever heard of a deafening quiet? Believe me, it is there. Besides, you can touch the stars at night when it's clear, and if you ever want to see God just go to the mountains. Some people marvel at cities and the architecture in buildings. I marvel at the architecture of a mountain peak in the mist, a lone spruce in a high meadow, a boulder in a clear mountain stream, aspen leaves that fall to the ground, and the plants and animals that call the mountains their home. Scared, naw, I never get scared. I just relax and become a part of it all."

I had climbed up to about 11,000 feet in elevation. The air was clean and crisp here and the timber was beginning to fade slightly. I had been to this place before with Dirk. In fact, it was one of our favorite places in the world. By climbing about 1500 feet more, I could look down on Emerald Lake, and by going over the saddle just ahead, I could see the mountains forever.

I found a flat area, put my pack on the ground, and shook out my sleeping bag. I did not have a tent. I rarely took one. I did have a waterproof bivy sack into which I put my light down-filled bag. It was perfect.

For a couple of days I cleared my mind, sorted things out in my journal, and took day hikes to the saddle and to the Emerald Lake overlook. It was peaceful there and gloriously beautiful.

Before dawn on the third day I finished my coffee and began the uphill climb to the Emerald overlook once again. This time I would select a different location. Why? I did not know. I only knew that I had been awakened by the tremendous urge to write about what I had seen two weeks ago while visiting the two-year-old crash site. I was following my heart. I would stop where I was compelled to stop and I would write what I was compelled to write. I moved swiftly up the mountain, following nothing but a voice inside me.

Just as the sun was rising in the east I found the spot that I knew had been chosen just for me. I sat, leaned back against a boulder, and took a drink from my canteen. I looked at Emerald. A low-lying cloud was hovering over a portion of it, well below where I was sitting. It was picturesque. I scanned the mountain below me and there were deer and elk seemingly everywhere. A marmot whistled at me from my right and I acknowledged his presence by whistling back.

It was time to write and I picked up my journal and began.

The time was growing closer now and Old Sly could sense it. He would shed his antlers soon and this year he wished it would hurry up and happen. He had never wished this before. He was tired. Losing all that weight that hung out on both sides of his head would feel good this year. His magnificent rack now sported eight points on either side.

The fall season had been hard and the winter was shaping up to be a bad one. In his entire life he had never faced anything as bad as this before. Many strong, young bulls had challenged him for his harem of cows and he had fended them off one by one. Most had succumbed to his posturing and threats. Others had been frightened of his bugle and raking of trees. Others had been scared off by his head tilt and appearance, but there had been three younger bulls that had responded to his threats with full-scale charges. It had been a difficult time. The first of the younger bulls was a five-pointer. Strong and agile was he as he had made the charge and managed to inflict some injury before Old Sly skillfully moved higher on the slope and leveraged him off a small knoll. In that battle he had taken an antler to the left shoulder and it had drawn blood, something he had not felt before in all his other battles. Maybe he had. There had been so many in his lifetime he just couldn't remember.

Fighting off the infection that came as a result of his first injury had taken its toll. He had been in a particularly weakened state when the six-pointer made his way into the little valley with threats of a battle. Try as he might to dissuade the youngster with his grunts and clear bugle, he had instinctively known that another battle was in the making. He had tilted his head back and moved his cows farther down the slope but, in his heart, he knew that it would do no good. The youngster was spoiling for a fight and he might just as well get it over with.

You could hear the crashing sound of the battle from over a mile away. As the two magnificent animals lowered their heads for charge after charge, every animal in the entire valley was aware of the showdown. Time and time again they had rammed together, each pushing the other backward for a time, then losing their momentum and being pushed. He had taken another antler on the left shoulder. Blood had trickled out, bathing his shoulder in crimson red.

That fight had taken all the strength he had left. Had it not been for his tactical positioning, he sensed he would have lost the encounter and been banished from his herd. It was a maneuver he had perfected in his younger days, when, as a five-pointer, he had won his first battle against the old herd bull he had challenged. In fact, the six-pointer had reminded him of the way he had been only a few years before. Cocky, confident, strong, and eager to get a group of cows of his own. The maneuver was carefully planned and involved letting his opponent get the upper hand for a moment as he went backward with his head turned to the left. As the ground fell away from his hind legs, he felt for the firmness of the uphill position on the other side of the draw and, when he felt it, he mustered all his strength and scrambled with his hind legs up the slope. At the same time he used all his strength to throw his head to the right, which had the effect of sending his opponent down the slope off balance. As he sensed the pressure toward him being released, he charged, using the full weight of his body to inflict damage. This had given him the position he needed. With the scrambling six-pointer totally broadside he charged, knocking the animal to the ground. It wasn't long until the fight was over and his opponent was on his way off the battleground and out of his valley.

Regardless, the battle had opened the cut once again and he felt weaker and weaker. In fact, the last battle for territory had come just two days after the battle with the six-pointer. Old Sly knew that had this new animal been as strong as the first two bulls he had faced, he would be the one leaving the battleground and his cows.

He was tired as he herded his cows for the long trip to the lower elevations. He sensed the storm approaching. Instinctively he knew there would be no more fights and no more cows for him next year.

In the lower parts of the valley he looked after his cows and made sure they were safe. Even with the new snow he knew his little herd would make it through the winter easily as there was plenty of browse this year.

Restlessly, he looked over his herd. Instinctively, Old Sly knew that he would never see the new crop of calves in the spring. He was tired and the injury was too serious. Still, he knew that his seeds would do their job and his offspring would be all over the mountain as they had been for the past eight seasons. He was proud of that.

As his herd mingled with other migrating elk in the peaceful valley, he felt a sense of accomplishment. The other herd bulls and younger bulls were there also. There were no fights. No posturing. It was a time of coming together for the elk. It was a time to prepare for the harshness of winter.

He could sense the others watching him as he moved about in the meadow. There was an acceptance there. They all seemed to know that he was ready.

He left the herd slowly and took the northern ridge, looking back on the nearly one thousand cows and bulls now congregated in the valley. He bugled and the sound of the bugle seemed to echo throughout the valley into some distant place and then reverberate back as if drawn by a magnet. He heard the answers from the valley from bulls of all sizes and ages. He heard the mewing of the cows and their calves, as they seemed to wish him well. He watched the scene below him for a few minutes, taking it in and savoring the sight.

Slowly he turned northward and began his trek in the snow to a place he knew he must go. There was no spring in his step. There was no hurry. This was a time for moving slowly, and he took the time to look around at things he perhaps had seen many, many times but had never really looked at. He stayed on the south-facing slopes as much as possible, knowing full well that he must conserve his strength for the final climb into the high mountain valley that would be his final resting-place.

He sensed he had to go there. It was as if he were drawn to this spot by some unidentifiable force. As the snow became deeper, he took more time. His breath came in gulps as the air thinned and he moved farther upslope. As he trudged through the snow that was

now up to his belly, he thought back over his life and
the events that had transpired. He remembered the
strange two-legged creatures that had come up on
him right after he had been born. While he lay under
the tree he had sensed their love for him. He had
watched sleepily as they had slowly moved about and
set up some mechanical things. He had heard a
strange clicking and a whirring noise and seen a
small red light. Mostly, though, he had heard the
whispers from men and had sensed the warm sensations of love and respect. He even heard their names.
The oldest was Jake, next was Dirk, and the youngest
was Colt.

He crossed a little creek and scrambled up the
other side into a small rockslide. He had been here
before many times. He rested for a minute and
recounted his next major experience with the
two-legged creatures. It had been some three years
since his first encounter and he had grown... really
grown. He now had six points on each side on his
beautiful antlers and was the strongest bull on the
mountain. He had heard a bugle well below him and
had answered the bugle. Two of the same creatures
that he had seen as a calf were creeping up the ridge
and one of them had a long strange-looking object
slung around his shoulders. He recognized the men as
Dirk and Jake. His mother had taught him to fear
these two-legged creatures that she had told him were
men.

"Stay away from them at all costs," she had
warned. "They mean to do you harm. They are
dangerous. If you smell them, run until you can
no longer smell them. Then run some more."

"But, Mom, they never hurt me before. In fact, they made me feel loved. They just watched me and sent me love," he argued.

"You stay away from them," his mother had warned. "They are dangerous."

He had sensed some danger from the men below, but mostly he had sensed something else. He sensed a struggle within the souls of the two men. He had ripped at a sapling with his antlers to show them who was boss of the mountain. He had witnessed them at close range as they whispered back and forth to one another and pointed at him. He recognized them as Jake and Dirk. Jake pointed the long strange-looking object at him. He had sensed danger. What was the object they were pointing at him? He wasn't sure. He had heard mention of an object like that before. He associated it with having a tremendous noise like a thunder strike. Sometimes after the noise he would not see some of his friends again. It was as if they had vanished.

More whispering between the two and the object was handed from Jake to Dirk, and once again the object was pointed toward him. Once again he felt danger. Soon it was handed back to Jake.

"Shoot him. He's the biggest bull in the area. A real trophy," Dirk had whispered.

"If you want him shot, you take my gun and shoot him," Jake whispered. "He is magnificent. Look at those antlers. He will drop the best calves this mountain has ever seen. I can't kill him. Here, you take the gun if you want him shot."

Once again he had sensed danger but was some-how not afraid. Somehow he knew that the struggle that was going on inside these two men would keep him safe, and he continued to bugle and rake the trees even though the men were just a short distance from him. He knew that he was one of the biggest elk in the forest and he also knew he was one of the toughest.

He watched them as one would point the object and then take it off its shoulder and give it to the other. Then there would be more whispering. Then the other would point the object, then more whispering. Finally he had heard one of the men say "Bang, bang," and he had taken off up the ridge. He had heard their laughter and he had sensed the same sense of joy as he ran. There was something nonthreatening about Dirk and Jake. He had been taught by his mother, father, aunts, and uncle to fear and stay away from the creatures at all costs, but these didn't seem to fit the mold.

He continued his journey. The snow was deeper now, and he trudged slowly upward, following the trees and trying to stay out of the deep snow. He once again stopped, feeling suddenly weak. As he rested, he remembered how many encounters he'd had with the three men.

Every year for the last seven, Dirk, Jake, and Colt had hunted him. They had followed him everywhere and he had enjoyed their chase. He had teased them by bugling and letting them get a glimpse of him, then circling around them and watching them look for him. He loved the game and he loved the men who pursued him so diligently.

He remembered his last encounter with Jake. It had been the most special event in his entire life. It was right after he had left the bachelor herd. He was by himself, looking for cows. As he had walked along the side of a ridge, he first came across the scent of the man he knew as Jake. Soon he saw him walking

through the forest. This time, however, he had sensed
something very different. First, he looked entirely different. He was a different color and seemed to be more
real than he had been at any time before. He sensed
that Jake was more tuned into the essence of the forest. Jake was, he sensed, totally at peace with the
world and totally unencumbered by any restrictions.

As he stood watching, he had sensed an overpower-
ing love — even stronger than his mother's love. He
hadn't moved and Jake moved toward him slowly, in
a nonthreatening way. He was not afraid. He
watched as Jake leaned over to pick some grass. He felt
him trying to communicate with him, both aloud
and silently, and he understood the communication.
Jake told him of his appreciation of him as the most
beautiful creature in the forest. He liked the feeling. It
felt good. It felt right. He and Jake stood watching
one another and Jake moved closer toward him, grass
in hand, and held out his hand toward him. He
sensed the joy and peace and love that the man possessed. There was no fear. He felt a part of Jake. He
knew Jake was a part of him. Closer and closer the
man had come. Stronger and stronger had been his
feeling of love. He saw the purple rings around the
man. They seemed to encircle his body. He felt warm
and alive. He sensed pain in the man and sent a part
of himself... a part of his soul... to Jake.

After a period of time he felt the need to move on.
At this point Jake had been just a few feet from him
with his hand out. The grass was in his hand. Slowly,
he had moved off, looking back at the man and the
aura of purple light that surrounded him. Instinctively he knew what he had encountered was very
special. It was the way it was supposed to be.

Old Sly moved slowly up the slope now, reflecting on
the many times that he had seen the two-legged

creatures and how he had enjoyed the relationship all his life. Even though he sensed danger more than once from men, he had never sensed danger from Dirk, Jake, or Colt. He respected them and they respected him. Oh, they had followed him. They had followed him over creeks, into draws, up mountains, on top of ridges, into dark timber, into aspen thickets, around springs, through brush, and into deep canyons. He had let them see him. He had talked to them. He had listened to them as they had talked to him and tried to trick him into coming closer. He had enjoyed all of it. It had been an experience that no other elk had ever had. Mostly, other elk had bad experiences with men. His had been a good one, and all the other elk used to ask him to tell his stories over and over and he did.

The fear of man was taught to each baby elk by their mothers. Still, Old Sly knew his love and respect for Dirk, Jake, and Colt and the love and respect he had sensed from them to him was sometimes almost overwhelming. He instinctively knew that his stories would be passed down from generation to generation and that his experiences would live on forever.

As he came out of the draw and moved through the tall ponderosa pine, he knew his journey was almost complete. He briskly stepped across the icy creek and up the slope to a spot he sensed was right for him. There he tramped the snow a little and laid down in the warm glow of the noonday sun. He was at peace with the world as he fell into a deep sleep.

By this time tears were streaming from my eyes and onto the paper. I lay the journal on a nearby boulder and stood, walked a short distance, and screamed. My body shook uncontrollably as I sobbed. I turned 360 degrees, threw both hands to the sky, and screamed again.

"Why?... Why?... Why?"

I sobbed then. For a long time I just stood there and cried. Then I heard the voice inside me as it said gently, "Finish the story, Jake. Finish the story. There's not much more. Finish it. You know what you have to do."

I moved slowly back to the boulder and sat down, picking up the journal. I knew what I had to do. It was just so difficult to write these last couple of sentences to the story.

> *It had been two years since the fateful crash of the little Cessna aircraft that carried Jake's best friends to their deaths on the mountainside in Colorado. Something had drawn him back to the spot. Something compelled him to go.*
>
> *He hiked in, not knowing what to expect, only following his heart. What he found astonished him.*
>
> *Only a short distance, and upslope from where the plane and mountain had met, Jake found the antlers and carcass of the bull elk known as Old Sly.*
>
> *Colt, Dirk, and Old Sly were together.*
>
> *Love has no boundaries.*

Chapter 12

"A man cannot be comfortable without his own approval."

Mark Twain

OFTEN I NAPPED in the mountain meadows while the warm sunshine regenerated my body. I'll never forget one day I was sunning and watching bumblebees pollinating the purple aster flowers. They looked bleached out in the harsh sun and I remember so well talking to them.

"I'm surprised at you little asters. You are not very pretty. I'm even surprised that the bee is finding you attractive enough to pollinate."

The sun bathed me in a blanket of warmth and I dozed off. I woke to a chilling wind and looked to the west where the mountain peaks were being painted by a glorious sunset. There was an array of colors there — purples, lavenders, grays, oranges, blues, and reds. Some afternoon clouds were touching the peaks and the sky was filled with beauty and mystery. It was a beautiful moment. I watched the sunset for a few minutes, then followed the flight of a bald eagle as it soared eastward into a full moon now creeping into the sky. It was spectacular. I followed the eagle's path northward until I could no longer see him. It was then I noticed something else. There was a neon glow coming from the meadow I was in. As I turned my head to the right it was everywhere in the meadow. To the left it was the same. I made myself stand and turned full circle. The glow stretched out over the meadow as far as I could see. It was alive with purple... not dull purple... bright, neon purple. Every aster flower in that meadow was glowing as they reflected their colors with the colors of the sunset. I dropped to my knees and prayed as I viewed the scene stretching out before me.

"Dear God, thank you for this moment. Thank you for allowing me to be here today to see this beauty. Thank you for showing me that nothing in your kingdom is ugly. Thank you for showing me that all things are beautiful in your world. Thank you for this beautiful lesson."

I stayed as if glued to that spot until well after dark, tears streaming down my face. They were tears of joy... tears of happiness... tears of wonder... tears of understanding.

Every night since I had left the trailhead I had slept under a beautiful clear sky filled with stars. This was the sixth night and I found myself wide awake at 3 A.M. I watched satellites move across the sky, and an occasional airplane. Shooting stars were everywhere, but they always are at two miles above sea level. I stuck a naked arm out of the down-filled mummy bag and felt the cold night air on my skin. I dug around for my coffee, pumped the valve on my WhisperLite, and lit it. As the flame leaped to life, the noise of the pulsing blue flame penetrated the silence on the mountainside. I poured some water from my plastic canteen into my aluminum pot and put it on the stove. As I pulled my arm back into the warmth of my sleeping bag I thought of my last few days in the mountains. It had been an incredible trip and I had done some great writing in my journal. Jeni and I would have plenty to talk about. We would discuss the strengths and weaknesses of staying in the Durango area as opposed to moving back to the Dallas metroplex.

The water came to a boil and I put a coffee bag in my cup and filled it full of boiling hot water. I loved those little bags. They were so handy in the mountains. As I lay there drinking my coffee and looking at the stars I was wishing I could share this moment and the one I had experienced in the meadow with Jeni. I would for sure tell her about it. Telling is not sharing, though, and I was wishing she were with me.

As I sipped my coffee I realized that I had what I came for, and, as usual, much more. I always had a difficult time leaving the mountains, but I knew that it was time to go. Jeni and I had some decisions to make and we needed to be about it. I couldn't just stay up here forever even though sometimes I wanted to.

The more I thought about her, the more I wanted to be with her. I wanted to share my "mountaintop" experiences of this week with her. At 3:30 I packed up and started down the long trail to the trailhead. The switchback trail I had come up was plenty tricky at night, but the full moon helped.

I never stopped for a rest that day. It was about fourteen miles to the trailhead but I was ready to see my Jeni and talk. There were a few other things on my mind too. I walked fast and made the trailhead at about 11 A.M. My blue pickup was covered in dust and I was determined to wash it before I rested.

When I got home Jeni warned me that I needed a nap first, that I needed some rest before I did anything. I was too stubborn. I was determined to wash that pickup. She stood on the staircase and watched and we talked as I washed. The bed was slick and full of soap.

Next thing I know I am falling out of the bed of that pickup. I struggle in midair to get my feet in under me, and when I hit you could hear the popping sound for at least one hundred yards. I screamed and looked at my right leg. My foot was turned 180 degrees from the way it was supposed to face. It was completely backward.

"Jeni, call 911 and get an ambulance. I have a compound fracture of my right tibia and it is bad," I instructed.

She had started down the stairs to where I was but turned immediately and ran back into the house, following my instructions. I looked again at my leg. It almost made me sick just to look at it. All my years in first aid told me that I would in all likelihood go into shock. I also determined that I needed to set the leg and splint it. I knew that the jagged bone would be dangerous if I tried to set it. It could cut an artery in my leg. I also knew that was a possibility if I did not set it. I made up my mind.

I grabbed my foot in one hand and my ankle in the other and applied traction in the direction of the foot. I turned it about 90 degrees. I screamed. I could not help it. I was covered in sweat and I looked at the leg again. It was sticking straight out to the side. I gritted my teeth and applied traction again and turned it once again. I screamed once again. It was a loud scream. Again, I could not help it. It hurt.

I took stock of the foot. It was back in place and I was covered in sweat. It had ceased to hurt. I knew, however, that I was in a great deal of danger of going into shock.

Jeni came barreling out the door. I could tell by the look on her face she was petrified.

"They are on their way!" she screamed.

I was totally calm and the pain had subsided. I knew that Jeni would need to know what to do so I very calmly told her.

"Baby, I have set the bone. Now I need some things and you need to help me. I need something comfortable to lie on as we wait for the ambulance. Bring me my Thermarest sleep pad. Second, I need something to splint this leg with. Third, I will need a blanket and something to prop my legs on so that I can keep from going into shock. Last, I need a couple of aspirin. Can you help me with that?"

She was back in a flash with everything I needed. I splinted the leg with her help and she helped me get comfortable while we waited on the ambulance. When they arrived about an hour later, I tried to tell them that they would have to keep my leg from moving in the ambulance. At the hospital the EMTs came into the room.

"Man, we had no idea that you had that kind of a break. We just saw your x-rays. You snapped that tibia half in two and twisted the fibula off. Why didn't you tell us it was that bad? You didn't even look like you were hurting."

Jeni was strong with the hospital staff in the selection of the doctor to fix my leg. After calling a friend who knew the orthopedic surgeons well, she picked Dr. Goodman. She stood her ground and told the hospital that she would take me out of the hospital if she were not allowed to use the surgeon that we wanted. She even told him, "Dr. Goodman, we have no insurance. I'm not sure how we will pay for this, but if you can't do this surgery then I'm taking him out of here right now."

The surgery was to put a titanium rod in the tibia starting at the knee and running to the ankle. It would require screws at both the knee and the ankle.

I was on crutches for four months during that time, but, after the stitches healed, Dr. Goodman allowed me to swim. He marveled at how well my pool exercise program worked in the rehabilitation process. It did not surprise me in the least. It all stemmed from

"Puff, puff, chug, chug... I think I can—I think I can—I think I can—I think I can..."

And God provided. As it turned out our automobile insurance policy had a clause that covered us completely. Just as he provided the grasshopper for the bird, he took care of us.

"I can't believe you're doing a triathlon just one year after they put that rod in your leg. Remember that guy we met in Durango who could not walk without a cane after the same surgery you had?" Jeni asked.

"Yeah, I remember," I said.

"It had been three years since they put the rod in his tibia and he could barely move. And here you are doing a triathlon. He also said he was still having a lot of pain with his. I never hear you complain about the pain."

"I don't have any pain. Never did have much. I had a great doctor."

"He had the same doctor. Dr. Goodman told me the operation was very similar."

"Maybe I had more 'want to' than he did," I said.

"I think you have more want to than anyone I've ever met," Jeni added.

It had been a year since my surgery and we were back in our home in McKinney.

"I also can't believe that we are nearly out of debt," Jeni added.

"I think it is all about focusing on your objectives. What do you think?" I asked.

"We are certainly blessed."

"That we are, Jeni darlin'. That we are."

And we were blessed. Jamie was a fantastic mother and I was very proud of her. She had played the cards she had been dealt and had come through like a champ. Equally important, Jamie had remarried. This time to a delightful man named Gene Carlson. Gene, an Alabama native, was living in Durango because he loved the outdoors. He had a winning smile and seemed to love Jamie and the girls. Jamie deserved some happiness and I was happy for her.

Jay was everything a father could ask for and much more. Aside from being a handsome man in his physical appearance, Jay had a certain charismatic quality that everyone could feel. He had a sincere love and compassion for people that was uncanny for a young man. He possessed a determination to succeed and owned his own business and was doing well financially. Everyone who came in contact with Jay was a better person for it. I was proud Jay was my son.

Jeni had taken a new job in counseling and loved it. Our home was wonderful. We bought a boat big enough to sleep on at Lake Texoma. Yep, the music was starting to play again around our house.

On May 31, 2000, we were sitting on our big chair in the living room watching a new reality TV program that was airing for the first time. I was totally intrigued with the show.

"I could do what those guys are doing," I said to Jeni.

"I think you could too. Of course, Jake Billingsley, I think you can do anything."

I watched the show *Survivor* religiously, pitting myself against every player in that first season. I understood the concept and I loved it. First, it was a physical competition. Second, it required people skills. I was good at both. It was absolutely perfect for me. I was physical, an outdoors person, and a people person. I knew I could do it. Interestingly enough, I watched every episode of *Survivor* in my old adventure hat. Jeni would smile as I prepared for each episode. It just felt right to wear it.

My adrenaline pumped and I felt my heart rate increase during the physical challenges. After the first season I was totally hooked. Without question I was a *Survivor* fan. When the first season ended, I was depressed. I could not wait for the second season to begin.

The first episode of *Survivor: Australia* aired on January 28, 2001. I was in front of the television, my beat-up old hat on my head, watching and learning. On the second episode, a contestant named Michael Skupin said that anyone over fifty would have a tough time with the physical part of the show. That statement really pissed me off. I was fifty-nine at the time and I knew I was tougher than anyone who had ever been on that show or anyone who would ever be on it. I screamed at the TV, "You haven't met me yet, Mike. Not only can I do that show, I can win it."

I was like a man possessed. At the CBS web site I found an application and the rules. I filled out the application for *Survivor 3* immediately, then read the rules. The application was to be accompanied by a video that answered the question, "Why do you think you can win on *Survivor*?" Since I had done tons of videography with Dirk and Colt, I felt pretty confident. Equally important, I had a good S-VHS camera.

I wrestled with determining how to get the attention of the casting director. I needed to submit something special in my video without making it look professional. I had tons of old VHS footage lying around, and I decided to combine new footage with the old VHS stuff I already had. Great. I bought an editing machine and learned to use it. It was a digital editor, much different from the old analog machines I had used in the past. The video could be no longer than three minutes, but I estimated that if I could not get their attention in the first fifteen seconds I would not have a chance.

At the same time I was concentrating on my video, I continued my workouts on the bicycle and in the swimming pool. I would be ready for any physical challenge. I wrote everything that could be a negative for me in my journal and set out to get rid of all the negatives. The fact that I was wearing contact lenses I figured was a negative, so I checked on the new Lasik surgery.

"I plan to be on that show *Survivor,*" I said, talking to the doctor.

"Good show. I imagine it is difficult to be cast for it," he answered.

"Yeah, but I will be there. Can you do this surgery on one eye only? I want to be able to see at a distance with my right eye and I do not want to have to wear glasses to read."

"We can do that and you will be happy with the results," Dr. Carter added.

I had it done but wasn't happy with the result. But the second time I could see crystal clear at a distance. It was perfect.

At night I would lie in bed and visualize about being on *Survivor.* It was the same type of visualization I used when I learned a new dive. I visualized every step I needed to take.

"You are like a man possessed," Jeni said.

"I plan to be on that show," I answered.

I sent in a great tape and waited patiently for the reply. The web site instructions indicated that it would be at least thirty days and that eight hundred contestants would be given an interview. I felt very fortunate that I was given one of the interviews but certainly did not have a "warm fuzzy" feeling about my chances of getting on the show based on my interview.

Everything made me nervous but especially the camera. I knew I did not do well in the interview. I was just too intimidated by the magnitude of it all, I guess.

"You blew that one, Jake," I said to myself. "You will have to do better next time or you'll never get on that show."

I sat right there in the parking lot, reached for my pad, and wrote down every interview question I had been asked. I wanted them handy. I figured I would have to do better next time. Then I called Jeni and told her the bad news.

"I'll bet you did better than you think," she said.

"I'm telling you, I blew the interview, but I'll do better next time," I said.

I immediately started work on my second video. New digital video cameras were on the market and I had to have one. I knew I would have to do something different in my second video, and, I hoped, better. Jeni seemed somewhat amused by my determination and perseverance, but I could tell she was not a true believer. *Survivor: Africa* aired and I watched, wishing I could have been one of the contestants.

My second video and application was complete months before the required date. I held on to it and sent it in two weeks prior to the deadline. I waited. Nothing. I watched the mail every day. Nothing. I was not going to be on *Survivor 4*.

I continued to visualize my being on the show every single night. I would lie in bed and watch myself on TV, competing and proving myself.

When it finally became apparent that I was not getting an interview, I began work on my third application and video. Jeni was becoming a bit perplexed by all of this.

I continued to shoot a good bit of my application footage in the woods. I would set up a tripod and do my thing in front of the camera. I could see if I liked the lighting, the background, the script, and, in general, the message. I wanted that message to be good.

My old cowboy hat had the rugged adventurer look that I wanted to portray and I wore it in all my videos. One hot day I had taken my hat off to review one of the short segments I had just recorded. I hung it on the branch of a tree. As I looked at the hat hanging there, I was suddenly struck with an unusual sensation… like having a light bulb go off in my brain. I was having what highly educated people would call an epiphany. The message I received was loud and clear.

People say that my old hat has character, and it does. The character stems from the many places it's been and the many adventures it has been through. It's weathered many a storm and protected me from snow, sleet, hail, rain, sun, and tree limbs. It dawned on me then that the old cowboy hat's character was my character. The shape of that hat came from being with me. Its shape came from the experiences we'd shared, the places we'd been, and the people we'd met together. Our character is directly related to those things that we have experienced and how we have reacted to those experiences.

The thought continued. The shape of our hat is determined by our attitude, desires, successes, and failures. The shape of our hat is determined by who we are and what we are about. It is our character. It is who we are. God gave us the ability in life to shape our own character. We can't help it if we are not pretty as a teenager, but if we are not beautiful at age seventy, it's our own fault. The shape of our hat can change or stay the same.

"Your character, Jake, is the authentic you... the genuine Jake," I heard myself say.

Everything we have done and will do in our lives shape who we are. All the choices we have made thus far in our lives have contributed to that shape. Not only that, each and every day that we are alive we are continuing to shape our hats. We shape our hats with our thoughts, our decisions, our attitudes, our choices, the people we are around, and how we choose to live our lives. The shape of our hats will be what we want them to be. What we have done in the past is a part of that shape. What will happen in the future will also have an effect. We will be shaping our hats every minute of every day.

That means if we don't like our life the way it is we can change it. In order to do that we have to dive out of the tree and go into the meadow with faith that God will provide the nourishment we need to form a better life. We have to take that first step of faith. We have to believe we can do it. We have to risk something with the faith that we will find a better life.

"Wow," I thought. "Risking and faith are almost synonymous. If we know the outcome before we try something, it is not an act of faith. When we say that we have faith that this or that will happen we are, in fact, taking a risk that it will happen. We have to risk to have faith. That's good stuff. So risk taking is not a bad thing. It's a good thing. It demonstrates our faith. For that reason, great love involves risk. Great achievement involves risk. Both require faith."

In that context, knowing we need to change something in our lives and not doing it because we are afraid is totally unacceptable. Staying in a bad relationship that cannot be fixed is unacceptable. Not fixing a relationship that can be fixed is unacceptable. Putting bad "stuff" in our bodies is unacceptable. Not liking ourselves is unacceptable. Not loving ourselves is unacceptable.

It's about living life to the fullest. It's about trying something we've never tried before. It's about self-study and learning about ourselves. It's about having respect, not only for others, but for ourselves as well. It's about giving all we have every single day. It's about helping others. It's about being the best we can be. It's about loving. It's about building relationships.

We have to believe in ourselves. We choose the shape of our own hats. If we have no self-confidence, we need to take the steps to get some. Self-confidence comes to a person who can look in the mirror every day and like what he or she sees. If we don't like ourselves, we need to take action. We are created in God's own image, for heaven's sake. How can we not have self-confidence? Some people are afraid to act confident because they are afraid that others will perceive them to have a big ego. There is all the difference in the world in a person who has a "big head" and one who is confident. Confidence is built one small step at a time... one success after another... one failure (while trying) after another. When we boil it all down, all we really ever have is our own self-confidence. That's it. If we have it, we can handle any situation or obstacle. Without it, we blame others when things don't go our way. Without self-confidence we become a poor substitute for the person our higher self wants us to be.

It dawned on me that all my life I had been building my character. The lessons from my mama reading, "I think I can... I think I can... I think I can..." is now a part of who I am. My father's teaching me that

I can have anything if I am willing to work for it is a part of me. My accepting responsibility for all my choices is a part of who I am. The lessons Mama and Daddy taught about respect for myself and others helped shape my hat. The Scout Laws are part of Jake. Understanding that sometimes not winning is a wonderful stroke of luck adds shape. Losing but keeping the lesson from the loss is character building. Being open to change is a part of who I am. Spending time alone and loving nature is me. Facing my fears is a part. Realizing when I have made a mistake and taking action to correct it helps define me. Understanding my strengths and weaknesses and setting objectives to be a better person helps build my character. Visualizing my life as I want it to be helps define me. Perseverance is a part of me. Seeking wisdom is a part of me. My love for my family is a part of the shape of my hat. Following love helped me define who I am. My trust in God is a part of me. Understanding what is important to me helps define me. Dirk, Colt, and Old Sly are a part of me. So are Jackie, Jeni, Jamie, and Jay, and everyone I have come in contact with. So are the books I have read and the movies I have watched.

It had been years since my naked sojourn into the backwoods of Colorado in search of answers. I had found some of those answers at that time. More by following my intuition. Still more by following love. The question as to "What is the shape of my hat?" had completely eluded me until that very moment. Building character is a process.

There was a second epiphany. It occurred to me that the game of *Survivor* was more about character, values, ethics, and morality than it was about the million-dollar prize money. "What would you do for a million dollars?" was the central theme.

Some would do anything to win. The "win at all costs" philosophy is a part of their makeup. They would lie, cheat, steal, and maybe kill to win.

To others there is a "win-win" philosophy. They will not give up their integrity for a million dollars.

Still others would not compromise their values for all the money in the world. They understand who they are and what they are about.

It became apparent to me that the game of *Survivor* was the ultimate test of the character of a person. I knew that my character had been tested and my hat shaped by the many obstacles I had faced and the many lessons I had learned. I knew that I would pass my own test in that game whether I won the million dollars or not. I also felt sure I would take that test.

Jeni became frustrated with me. "When are you going to come back into the real world and give up this obsession about being on *Survivor*?" she asked.

I pretended not to hear. Sometimes it was better just to let Jeni vent her frustration and pretend not to hear. Doing that, of course has a consequence. She thinks I have a hearing problem.

"I said when are you going to go back to work, Jake?" she spoke louder this time.

I wasn't going to push my luck too far. I answered her this time. "You just don't understand, Jeni darlin', I'm going to be on *Survivor*; CBS just doesn't know it yet."

"Puff, puff, chug, chug... I think I can—I think I can—I think I can..."